Britain's Premier Spa

Founded A.D. 54

Abounding in antiquarian and other interests, beautiful city set in delightful country · ·

The Grand Pump Room

Music thrice daily throughout the year, Tennis, Golf, Bowls, Boating and other outdoor sports are available, and there is an unusual choice of enjoyable motor excursions in every direction.

Roman Vessels for Drinking the Waters

The Book of Bath, Hotel and Apartment List, Baths Tariff and all information from John Hatton, Director, The Pump Room, BATH. If desired the Director will gladly assist anyone requiring accommodation.

Prior Park and Bridge

GLASTONBURY

THE "ENGLISH JERUSALEM"

Interior of Glastonbury Abbey (temp. Henry VII).

GLASTONBURY

THE HISTORIC GUIDE TO THE
"ENGLISH JERUSALEM"

BY THE LATE

REV. C. L. MARSON, M.A.

formerly Vicar of Hambridge, Nr. Taunton

Arms of Glastonbury Abbey.

*With Sketches by H. S. Stewart, and other
illustrations*

THIRD EDITION
THIRTEENTH THOUSAND

THE GEORGE GREGORY BOOK STORE
8 GREEN STREET AND 1 BROAD STREET, BATH
LONDON: SIMPKIN, MARSHALL, HAMILTON, KENT & Co., LTD.
1925

THE publisher desires to acknowledge his indebtedness to Mr. F. Bligh Bond, F.R.I.B.A., for the use of his picture of the restored interior of the great church; also to Messrs. Parker and Son, of Oxford, for permission to reproduce the illustrations on pages 17, 20 and 22; and to the late Mr. Hulbert, of Glastonbury, for courteously allowing the use of several of his pictures.

PRINTED IN GREAT BRITAIN
AT THE PITMAN PRESS, BATH

PREFACE

IN presenting a short outline of a splendid subject, the writer has been guided by one chief principle, namely that of selecting what is likely to interest the sympathetic visitor. So far from rejecting tradition with the customary scorn, it seems more reasonable to admit its value, at least as great evidence, unless there is greater evidence to outweigh it. To make a summary of conclusions is a dangerous task, especially when so many hasty and hasty-tempered controversialists are in the field, and the theses have rather to be nailed to the door in brief, than be set forth at length with full reference and support : but the theory which makes so many generations of our people into fools and forgers is curtly rejected here. That is rather the theory which demands the greater evidence, than one which beholds these generations, as men who were at least as honest as ourselves and were more filled with those dreams of good, which belong to the powers which cannot die.

C. L. M.

DEDICATION

TO the memory of the many great Christians, who from this ancient Island beheld the Land that is very far off, who by their lives brought that vision nearer, whose prayers have been and are still the best wealth of the whole Church, even in the days when there is no open vision.

CONTENTS

ILLUSTRATIONS

ix

CHARLES L. MARSON

A MEMOIR

THERE is so little in bulk to tell of who Marson was while he lived among us. There were hundreds of pieces of his which he threw out into this or that journal of the day, and which all speak with the same brilliant vividness of phrase as his *Huppim and Muppim*. For he had the rare gift of literary distinction. Whatever he wrote, told. It had style, it had directness, it had keen intellectual precision, and it had inimitable charm. He had a real mastery with his pen. A very fine judgment found for itself instinctive expression in the most felicitous phrasing. And, then, in and out and round about everything that he wrote, there played the most delightful humour—ironic, perhaps ; provoking, often ; " naughty," sometimes, and most undiplomatic: yet always real, invincible, delicious. It was a dangerous gift, and he was not too wise in its exercise. But it was humour that belongs to the very heart of things.

I do not know enough of his earlier days to say when he first found himself. He made his mark very quickly in those days at Petersham, but he had not then arrived at what became his typical career. Out there in the colonies, he became what we all knew afterwards at home. He came back in full possession of his gifts. But though there was a quick recognition of his brilliancy, we never gave him his rightful opportunity. We did not really take a right estimate of his rich and wide studies. His beautiful little book on *The Psalms at Work* is just an index of the width of his reading, and of his sympathies. But we were content to laugh at his jibes and jokes ; and we were very much afraid of his wit, and we took him on his lighter and more perilous side ; and he, perhaps, allowed us to do so too much, and loved to confound our respectabilities, and to startle our pomposities, and to shock our conventions, and to provoke our silly indignation.

So we never understood him, or took a right measure of his work. No doubt, it was not very obvious where to put him, or what to make of him. So we left him to drift into jobs that were only partially his, and gave him many a hard time, and little stimulus for study and production. *He had a deep love for the poor, of a singularly Christ-like intensity, venerating them as the true people after God's own heart.* He saw them exactly as they really are ; he had none of the illusions about them which come from pity and condescension. Just as they are in themselves, he found them real and lovable. *He sat at their feet.* Gradually, he found his way into the hearts of the peasants, and learned to pay them the same honour. His little book of *Silhouettes* is exquisite in its natural instinctive portraiture of the village characters.

He was himself, to those who understood him, the most lovable of men. His letters to his friends are perfect, in their intimate fun and their playful charm.

So we let him live out his days in his far-away country vicarage. He had his home joys, and he knew how to put them to use. But there were powers in him which asked for a fuller exercise than we ever found for them. And, now, we can but gather together the broken fragments that witness to the richness of the feast from which they are left over.

He had the force and the charm about him of a quivering flame. There might be peril in its flickering tongue, but that only added to the joy of its fire and its illumination. He did us all good by his quickening touch. He loved, and was loved. Now, after feeling life keenly, he is in the peace which he desired.

R.I.P.

HENRY SCOTT HOLLAND.

(*Reprinted by permission of the Society of SS. Peter and Paul, Ltd.*)

FATHER MARSON

PERSONAL REMINISCENCES
BY
William Harvey Maidlow, M.D.

CHARLES LATIMER MARSON left us on 3rd March, 1914, and those of us who knew him feel his presence amongst us to a degree almost strange, but certainly pleasing. He was interested in so many people and things, such a kind friend and critic.

I believe nothing would have pleased him better than to figure in another volume of *Village Silhouettes*, indeed he has drawn himself on the frontispiece of his book.

At this lapse of time, only a feeble impression can be given of him, yet what a pleasant sketch a physician friend could portray, were he able to write impersonally. But you can't write impersonally of one you love—to do so is banal,—and I suspect this is the reason why there has been no sympathetic story told of this beloved and eminent priest. There isn't enough objectively to write very fully about ; and subjectively he transcends one's powers. He is kept as a sacred memory, hardly, indeed, to be talked about.

I met him, for the first time, in a cottage where he was blessing the medicines an aged woman was about to take. There was never any doubt that this increased its value. He would smile at us medical people. We liked, he would say, to think it was all our medicines that did good, but it's not these, it's the person and the atmosphere and the faith in you that do most, would you but realize it. He liked us if we worked well for his villagers. He was fond of all conscientious work, however much he jested. He wrote to me : " We must not lose faith, we in our priestcraft, you in your leech-craft, thereby bringing us nearer to each other than we dream." He had seen and performed faith-healing among lunatics, the dying and diseased, and drunkards, but leechdom (a favourite expression of his) was part of it, too. So we were not to despair. It is all, he said, rooted and grounded in the unseen.

What gentle reproofs he used to administer and how valuable ! I remember being very peevish at being called from cottage to cottage. He told me all about the behind-scenes life of his villagers and submitted these facts to my "*waspship*." Who would not be ashamed, or feel how silly was irritability !

He believed in fresh herbs, and I often met him riding his Rozinante sort of pony himself, like Don Quixote, searching for them. He would clothe my dry facts with romance and pleasure.

Sometimes he would show his skill in painting, painting scenery for his *Shepherd's Play*, painting Madonnas. There is, by the roadside in front of an inn, one of his signboard achievements now recently restored. On one side a lamb, the state you enter that hostel, on the other a lion's head facing—that's how you leave. He knew where to find a pike in the neighbouring stream, and as he fished he thought of Isaac Walton and the gentle Donne. His book on Walton is probably somewhere in manuscript. He started a museum for the Church school where he would bring gleefully something he had acquired. This should be remembered.

To Marson, I am convinced, we owe the resuscitation of Somerset folk-song. They are sung now in the Hambridge school. No one about there thinks of them as aught but his discovery. The music is a secondary feature to words in these ballads.

He loved the teachers no less than the taught, laughing perhaps at the "Huppim and Muppim" learning. There never was so loyal a supporter of the teachers than he. Many hold treasured letters from him, and inspectors, with whom he enjoyed tilting, remember him certainly without animosity.

Folk did not always attend church, but he was welcomed everywhere in his village. That church-bell would ring for worship, even had he to ring it painfully alone. The poor knew they had but to ask and he would help if he could. His parsonage was more than once the sanctuary for vagrants and the distressed. I have seen him leave personal friends and social functions where he seemed happy to carry out his almost self-ordained work. Poor himself, he made himself poorer, except in soul, by his many gifts. He once said he thought all riches were unjustly obtained. He didn't mean dishonourably obtained, but that there were needless and disproportionate differences in this world at least. This was in his old Fabian days, days when he contributed his racy articles in the *Commonwealth*. It has been said one never quite knew when he was jesting. I think he sometimes did put forward views to see how they

could be controverted and he would supply the answer
in a sort of Socratic method.   He enjoyed a tilt with
the pompous   I once saw certain clerks " jump " when
a marriage licence was dawdled over—the rather care-
worn looking Oxford man wondered if they " treated
the poor like this."

Yet, it must not be supposed for one moment that
his life consisted of quips and surprising versatility. He
loved and upheld and had faith in his main work in
life.   The little church of St. James-the-Less was the
holy ground for careful teaching—brilliant suggestions
from the pulpit, teaching and thought carried by him
to all the cottages—and for dignified ceremonial service
enriched by his own inspiring and fascinating person.
The worshippers understood it and still do, and their
Gregorian chants and music have become traditional for
earnestness and reverence.   He would order the full
diapason of the Creed of St. Athanasius, which he could
justify and fight for.   Indeed, his heart was in his work,
he believed all he taught, he was an ornament and a
light in his work, a man to follow, a fighter, a leader,
but ever kind and gentle to sinner and sceptic.

His books are well known.   His *Glastonbury*, whatever some archaeological failings, has brought many to
Avalon and through Avalon to higher thoughts.   It
will hold a place as a standard booklet.   The " Psalms
at Work " has been freely copied by others.   I know
many who read it in sickness, and like me read it after
and before a church service.   *Village Silhouettes* is
delightful.   Silhouetting was a hobby of his.   St. Hugh
of Lincoln was one of his heroes: he makes the

Saint live   Carthusians, young and old, must go to Witham.

The last scene was sad. His chronic asthma, which he would never allow to be treated seriously—we all tried to help him, lay and medical friends. He would scoff at treatment for his " poor carcase "—ended in acute heart failure. I remember I couldn't bear to stand by and see him suffer. He refused sedatives, preferring, like the speaker in Browning's " Prospice "—

> I would hate that death bandaged my eyes, and forbore
> And bade me creep past.
> No ! let me taste the whole of it, fare like my peers
> The heroes of old.

He was ever a fighter, and fought his last fight, " the best and the last "—for him, perhaps, but not for us, then.

Perhaps I looked vexed or pained : " Don't be an ass, go and fetch the nurse you say you want. How is William Marson ? " (my son, his godson) were the last words to me.

We were allowed to see him lying in his vestments, lying like a warrior taking his rest. If ever there was a saint in modern life, a saint who knew his own frailties, who sympathised with and tried to help the sorrows, sins and weaknesses of others, that saint was Charles Marson.

He lies in Hambridge Churchyard, with his face towards the west, as if gathering his eastward-looking flock. On his tombstone are these words—

> So he fed them with a faithful and true heart.
> *Psalm* 78.

EDITOR'S NOTE

THE Rev. Father Marson was born 16th May, 1859, at Woking. After Ordination, he lived at Morrison's Buildings, Whitechapel. He held curacies at St. Jude's, Whitechapel, St. Agatha's, Shoreditch, and was Rector of Orlestone, Romney Marsh, for three years. His strong Christian Socialist opinions, always so frankly and eloquently expressed, raised him up friends and enemies everywhere. He went to Australia in 1889 and was married to Miss Clotilda Bayne at St. Andrew's, Walkerville, Adelaide, South Australia, on Corpus Christi day, 1890. He returned to England in 1892, and after three London curacies, was given by Lord Rosebery in 1895 the living of Hambridge, where he died 3rd March, 1914. His only son, John Charles (b. 1896) was killed in action in Gallipoli, on the summit of Chunuk Bair, 8th August, 1915. Father Marson's daughter, Mrs. Stanley Gaster, survives him, she has a daughter Mary, and a son, John Marson Stewart Gaster, being Father Marson's grandson.

Mrs. Marson, his widow, sends me the above particulars. This lady lives at 86 Oakwood Road, Golder's Green, London, and works as a Coach, and London County Council Lecturer.

G. G.

THE HISTORIC GUIDE TO GLASTONBURY

PRE-CHRISTIAN GLASTONBURY

THIS quiet little town holds in her heart the romance and pain of English history, from the earliest days to which induction can point, to our own time. Glastonbury is England's epitome : but the very phrase is ineffective, for as there is no one name for the mother island of many races, so there is no one name for the Isle of Avalon, which has seen them come and go without ever losing her identity We have to use the modern names for both.

Glastonbury was an ancient fortress and treasure house, long before it was the English Jerusalem, the Mother of Saints, the grave of kings, and the second Rome. Though it now lies fourteen miles inland, yet it was once an island, at the back of a large oozy estuary (the Uxella). This lake or swamp—it must have been both—was dotted with islands, of which Brent Knoll is the highest and Wedmore the largest. From the land side there were two approaches, one from West Pennard through Ponter's Ball and the fortress of Edgarley, the other and more difficult across the Brue from Street. We may safely add that the place was defended by a palisade and the Tor was its citadel. Since in the XVII century the floods came up to St. Benignus Church, the palisade must have run somewhere about that point, and thus the town would be about a mile in mean diameter.

A treasure city and emporium needed to be on a large
scale, as the working population who lived on the islands
about might need to take refuge there, at a pinch.
These inhabited the lake villages discovered and to be
discovered. The houses were low mud and wattled huts,
thatched with reed, more or less circular, the hearth in
the centre, with slabs of stone or timber at the threshold.
Many of these British houses were washed with lime and
had woodwork of oak, willow, alder and beech. There
is no trace of any savage period here. It was the meeting
place of men of many civilizations, and consequently
shared in many methods, as we should expect. The
Kymry were here over a thousand years B.C., and
it seems to have been they who began the great camps
and the intersecting roads which united the chief centres
of Somerset. They named our rivers with Celtic names,
and it was with them that the Phœnicians traded.[1]
The chief exports from Britain were corn, cattle, fabrics,
gold, silver, lead, and *lapis calaminaris*. Of these lead
was by far the most used and most important in the early
world. Festus Avienus learnt from a Greek author of
about 260 B.C. that the Tartesii were used to come for
trade to England for lead and tin. " Tarish and the
isles " really means Cadiz, possibly the Scilly Islands, and
certainly Somerset. From the Land's End to the combined mouths of the Parrett, Brue and Axe, there is no
safe anchorage for ships, and this then is the key of
West Britain. The treasure city was protected by three
camps at Bleadon, Brent Knoll, and Otterhampton, and
since the Brue was formerly nine feet deeper than it is

[1] And possibly even the Phrygians.

now, the great vessels could come up with pottery, bronze, salt, and other commodities from Cadiz to the very heart of the waterways to unload.

About the time of Plato new Gallic tribes poured into England. From Burgundy and Belgium the Belgic Ædui conquered the land between the Avon and Parrett, making Bath, Glastonbury and Ilchester their chief cities. When the Roman arms shattered the Punic powers the Ædui continued the trade but diverted it to Vannes, in Brittany, where the place names and the remains in the Museum give evidence of the connection. This explains why the Britons helped the Veneti against Cæsar and how the victor in the great sea battle cleared the channel for his sanguinary surveys. The opening of the Spanish mines and Cæsar's conquests must have dealt a blow to the trade which flowed from Glastonbury through Vannes to the Rhone. It was the disappointing pearl trade which drew Cæsar to the West, and " most of the merchant ships now go to Kent." Consequently the Glastonbury trade must have been at a low ebb at the time of that great hush when the Son of God was made flesh.

In A.D. 43 the Claudian conquest began. Perhaps none of the dominations Glastonbury has seen so changed the face of the land. Camps rose, bridges spanned the rivers, above all great roads were made, which were the furrows in which the seeds of the Faith were sown. Ruthless press work, " wearing out the inhabitants," was the process, and we owe many of our Somerset roads to that very Vespasian who fulfilled Christ's prophecy by the destruction of Jerusalem.

One road was driven from Bridgwater along the Polden hills and passed through Wirrial hill to Glastonbury. Another along the southern slope of the Mendip from Uphill to Old Sarum, and thence to Southampton, was obviously designed to tap the lead trade. Bath became the social centre and Camelodunum the military centre of the colony. Since the metal trade was the most important source of gain, and this was centred in the Mendip mineries, Skinner's theory that the fixed and chief Camp of Camelodunum or Camelot was near Camerton seems more reasonable than the Colchester theory more generally accepted, which divides the social from the military centre by an impracticable track. The fierce revolt of Boadicea came next, with the massacre of the legions, and Suetonius Paulinus in one act struck Britain back to her old tameness. A new Governour, Petronius, was sent to heal the old sores, and the tides of conquest rolled to the North again, leaving Avalon now an open town, with perhaps some crumbs of the trade derived from the security and energy which followed the eagles ; but the share the Druid worship (centred at Stanton Drew) took in the late rebellion caused that religion to find no favour in the eyes of the imperial masters of Somerset. The conciliating Governour gave over this now less important part of the land to a puppet, King Arviragus, who found the island depressed and partly depopulated.

The visitor will find small fragments only of these periods. In the Museum are flints, bones, and rude pottery of the Kymry, who were driven off into Ireland. A small boat, bone horse bits, bronzes, whorls, weavers' combs, pottery with Phœnician influence, imported beads, and a host of curiosities from the lake village, serve to tell of the Ædui. There are plenty of Roman remains. Many place names recall these various rulers. Mendip is from a Semitic god Meni. The Brue (or swift river), the Parrett (meaning four), Wirrial (gweirio, to make hay) are examples of Celtic names. The Romans have left streets, strats, and " casters " scattered over the map. Even Ushant, Uxcellantis insula, is connected with the Uxcella or Axe ; but, on the whole, the small débris of great periods make controversy easy and conviction hard.

BRITISH CHRISTIAN AVALON

IN A.D. 63 St. Joseph of Arimathæa was sent by St. Philip from Gaul (possibly Galatia and France too) with some companions into England. After some repulse in North Wales, he landed at Bridgwater and came up the new Roman road, halting outside the half-deserted town on Wirrial Hill. He had known and served the Son of God, witnessed His resurrection, endured persecution for His sake and learnt by vision that He was more than Elias, that He had harrowed hell and burst the brazen gates asunder. St. Joseph was a married man and brought his son with him.[1] With him he carried two silver cruets with the precious Blood and Water washed from our Saviour's wounds, which

[1] Joseph also, from whose race King Arthur claimed to be descended.

cruets were buried with him in the sacred cemetery and
are some day to be discovered. Arviragus welcomed
the new settlers, and finding them neither Celtic nor of
the Druid faith, gave them land and leave to settle.
St. Joseph's staff grew into the holy thorn on Wirrial,
which certainly is a Levantine variety, and one which
has an immense vitality about it. For 14 years out of
17 it has decorated St. John's Altar with its flowers at
Christmas, and keeps fresh for a long time when
plucked.

There is an immense weight of authority from the
Fathers that the bounds of the West, Britain, received
the Faith from the first disciples, and those Fathers
(*e.g.*, Origen, Jerome, Eusebius, Theodoret, etc.) the
most careful and critical of all. The British writers,
Melkuinus and Gildas, have perished, and the old book
of the Graal is no more : but Leland found the first in
the Abbey library, and there seems no reason to doubt
that the belief in St. Joseph's mission was current in
Britain before the Saxon conquest. Arguments from
the silence of Bede show anachronism, for he was of
another kingdom. The charters do not mention the
story, for the holy men of old thought more of the Faith
than of the channel which brought it ; and the visions of
the Redeemer Himself to St. David and of His Mother
to King Arthur were more important even than the works
of the immediate followers. St. Joseph and his friends
built of mud and wattle the first Christian Church, not
only first in England but in the world. He built it
of mud and wattle, thatched with reed in the style of
the land, and made it 60 feet long, by 25 wide. There,

in the Eastern fashion, with Greek rites, a Greek Easter, and Greek ordinations,[1] the disciples lived in their separate huts, and worshipped in this lowly dwelling. Even if St. Paul and Simon Zelotes visited them, the mission was a rushlight only in the surrounding darkness, and although Tertullian says that the Faith was spread where the arms of Rome could not penetrate, yet it spread only with small and twinkling fires, for a century later there was certainly a strong revival of Druidism, which caused the Senate to class that religion among the *cærimonia illicita.*

Here must be told shortly the story of the Sangreal, which, if not history, has made much history and has inspired great poets for many centuries with dreams of good, drawn from " the holy isle of Avylyon."

While the earth was still void, there was war in heaven, and Satan led the rebel angels against the throne of God. In his crest was a shining ruby, the rallying point of all his soldiers, and this ruby St. Michael smote out with his flaming sword. It fell into the dark seas of the empty, formless earth. When Creation lit up the world it shone in the caverns of the sea and was fashioned by the sea-folk into a wondrous cup which no man knew of, until Solomon saw it by divination, and he sent and fetched it by the demons who were his slaves. When Solomon died, no one knew of its fate until his greater Son used that cup in the first Mass, for the chalice of His blood. In the large upper room it was seized by the soldiers and given to Pilate, who handed it to St. Joseph of Arimathæa ; and it was one of the

[1] Nennius.

vessels used to wash the sacred Body before It was put in the new tomb. It was by this marvellous cup that Joseph was kept alive and delivered from prison and he bore it with him in all his travels. When he died, it was laid up in King Peschour's treasure-house on Chalice Hill ; but the impure and defiled could never then behold it. Now, when anyone saw it, six candles first appeared, borne in by unseen hands, and a lovely silver altar was spread. Then came the cup draped in white or red samite, covered with the sendony or napkin which the Saviour gave to St. Joseph. Whosoever beheld that cup was glorified with the Holy Ghost, and if he might kiss it he was healed of all wounds and sickness. But now it is in Sarras, the spiritual city, where it is to be sought and found with all the other greatest treasures of earth, which also spring from the conflicts of heaven.

St. Joseph died, but his body has never been found, although tradition says that it lay near King Arthur's tomb. In 1345 John Blome obtained a patent to look for it, on the strength of a dream, but he found nothing. There is no mention of the relics of St. Joseph in John of Glastonbury in 1400, or in the Cottonian MSS. list, and though Pynson and Wynkin de Worde both printed lives of St. Joseph and record miracles wrought on those who asked for his prayers, they mention no relics, nor do any later writers. [1] It has been reserved for a Canon of Wells to foist a forgery upon the devout sons of St. Benedict and then unmask it. But the fact that there was no such forgery is surely sufficient evidence of their good faith.

[1] *e.g.*, Sanders, Cressy, Reyner, Fuller, Collier, etc.

In A.D. 179, at the petition of King Lucius, when Druidism was proclaimed, two Christian teachers came from Rome, Phaganus and Diruvianus. They travelled from Surrey and restored the little Church of the Mother of God and also built a monastery and chapel of St. Michael on the Tor ; after which, in the ages of persecution, there comes a blank in the story. The Mother of Saints is unlikely to have been spared, and the old church for a time became a lair of wild beasts. The inhabitants were killed or fled, so that for a little it seemed as though the cause was lost ; but the light often blown out seems to have been as often rekindled, and the edict of toleration under Constantine found the little church still in use. His maternal grandfather, King Hoel, indeed, was buried in the Grave of Saints, showing that the desertion was only temporary.

Under the strong rule of Rome the Britons became quickly unmanned by luxury and vices unknown before, but Glastonbury was, perhaps, still happy in its primitive simplicity. A century after the edict of toleration the Roman grasp was relaxed and the great wall stormed. The agony that fell upon Britain was felt less in the West than in the East ; but it was an agony that fell upon base minds. With effeminacy of living came an insolence of thought which produced the Pelagian heresy. This denied heredity and the social *nexus*, and so by implication the need of Christ's Society the Church. The Christians of Roman Britain were vexed by controversy within and the assault of the barbarians without, but Glastonbury seems not to have needed the reclamation of Germanus of Auxerre and Lupus of

Troyes. But near about the time that Vortigern called in
the terrible Saxons and the East was full of trouble, the
venerable St. Patrick came from his Irish mission to
end his days in the faithful island. He found twelve
orthodox Catholics here.[1] Over these he presided for
the last years of his life. Here he died and was buried
on the right side of the old altar. The constant visits
of Irish pilgrims to his shrine had great and good effects
upon the life and learning of the place, for Ireland was
in the van of art and learning. After St. Patrick and
his successor Benignus, " a cloud of forgetfulness veils
even the names of many abbots "—what else can we
call them ?—except three,[2] and we pass to the days
when King Arthur " left a name to be glorified in a song
of wonder and woe." He has the praise of staving off,
for many years, the ruin of his falling country. He
was only a boy when (c. A.D. 500) Cerdic's ship sailed
into the Parrett, but both history and legend connect
him with the place. Here he besieged the island to
recover Guinevere and she was restored to him by the
mediation of Gildas, the hermit of the Steep Holm.
Here his sword Caliburn was forged. Here he had his
vision,[3] and got the badge of our Lady, which nerved
him for his greatest of twelve battles, Bradbury, in
A.D. 250 Here he was carried to die after his last fight,
and here he was buried. If from the dawn of chivalry

[1] Their names, which may mean something to Celtic Scholars,
are given as Brumban, Hiregaan, Bremwal, Wencreth, Banttomeweng, Adelwolred, Lothor, Wellias, Breden, Swehoes Hinloernus, and Hyn.

[2] Worgret, Lademund, and Bregored.

[3] See page 81.

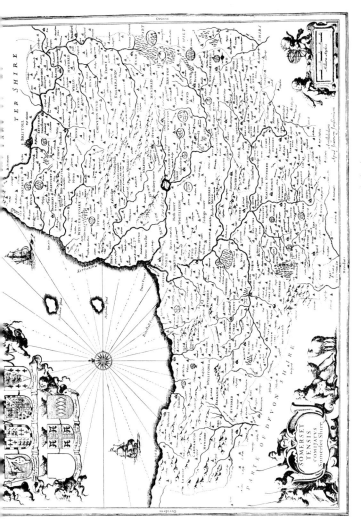

Robert Morden's Map of Somerset (1630).

See pages 1–5.

Arch of St. Thomas's Chapel looking into the Choir.
See page 24.

to the poets of our own age he has been a hero of romance, it is the romance of Avalon which has moved the world Perhaps there may be more of history even in Malory than some suppose ; and Launcelot du Lac may have followed indeed the dead queen's corpse from Amesbury to Avalon, but the beautiful tale is at least the mother, if not the child of historic truth, because of its great inspiration.

While Cerdic, Cenric, and Ceawlin were slowly fighting their way to the kingdom of Wessex and subduing it, Glastonbury still kept the Faith, which was by no means quenched even in these dark days. At this time St. David came to worship at so renowned a shrine, and he came with seven bishops prepared to consecrate the old church, which dated before any such ceremony ; but our Lord appeared to him in person and gave him a wound in the hand, in token that this was not to be,— a wound which was as wonderfully healed next day at the Mass.[1] St. David also gave the great sapphire to the altar, which was looted by Henry VIII and may possibly even now be among the Crown jewels of England. St David also built another church to the east of the old church, which was commemorated by the Galilee of later times.

When St. Augustine came in A.D. 597 there was still a strip of British kingdom jutting into Wessex, Malmesbury, Bradford and Glastonbury being its chief places, the last being the final base of the dwindling British power. Impressed with its fidelity and strength, Paulinus

[1] In later days, King Edgar brought relics of St. David to Glastonbury.

c (12 pp.)

of Rochester came here and cased the old church with
boards and lead, thus proclaiming that the Roman
mission worked not in rivalry, but to support and fulfil
the work of the British Church in its war with Saxon
heathenism. In 634 a new mission from Rome, under
Birinus " preached baptism " to the West Saxons.
Cynegils, the king, received the message and made an
alliance with King Oswald. It was just in time ; for
his son Cenwalk stormed the strip of land, fought two
great battles at Bradford and Pen, chased the Britons
to South Petherton and was lord of all the country north
of the Parrett by 658. Thus the island was saved, for
Cenwalk had been bred a Christian, and listening to
Archbishop Theodore (the Greek mediator between
Roman and British worship) he approached the spot
with reverence. Although he granted two hides of
land, he naturally insisted that a Saxon monk should
be made ruler over the monastery. Thus Glastonbury
became English, and got its newer English name, being
Ynswtryn, or woad island before,[1] or Avalonia, apple
land. It is hard to extract either derivation from either
name, but if there is any place where tradition should
have weight, it is surely here ? Glastonbury is said to
be the Saxon's translation into Latin of Ynswtryn,
glastum being woad ; but Adam de Domerham tells us
a tale of Glasteing, a British chief from the north, who
followed his old sow to Wells and found she had come
by the Sugewege to the old church apple tree. Therefore we have no need to accept or invent any false god,
such as Glast, to account for the name by anachronism.

---

[1] The *Genista tinctoria* is still to be found there.

The monk or hermit of this British period shaved the fore part of his head, wore leather next the skin, and had a white cowl, with a staff and a girdle. These anchorites lived in separate small mud hovels, fed upon bread and salt, drank water or milk, grew their own corn and were left much to their own devices. Some acted as schoolmasters. The nuns lived together and wore white gowns with white hoods. They kept Easter on the day of the full moon as " it had been kept and handed down by St. Philip the Apostle,"[1] without regard to the day of the week. This is one of the many matters which confirm the tale of St. Joseph being commissioned by St. Philip.

ENGLISH GLASTONBURY

THE British monastic custom—it was hardly a rule— did not long survive under the Saxon conquest, for in 688 the great pious king Ine came to the throne. He was seventh in descent from Cerdic, and as his house had received the Faith from Birinus he favoured the Latin rite. From the first he was keenly interested in Church matters, and at the last forsook the world and his crown, and died a holy man in Rome. He built a minster to the east of St. David's Church, the seed of the Great Church of SS. Peter and Paul of later days. He established the right of sanctuary, that makeshift of mercy in fierce ages. He built a monastery and

[1] Polycrates' Ep. to Victor, Eusebius, V. 22.

gathered together the hermit monks. He erected at
least one of the two stone obelisks to mark the graves of
many noble dead. He translated to the place the relics
of St. Indractus and his seven friends, who were Irish
pilgrims to St. Patrick's tomb murdered at Shapwick
because the flash of their brass-topped staves was
mistaken for gold. He endowed the monastery with
XXI hides of land, in addition to Arviragus' XII hides. [1]
He confirmed all previous grants, freed the Mother of
Saints from all exactions, such as forced labour and
conscription ; gave the Abbey primary jurisdiction
over all cases, freed it from the interference of bishops
and secular princes ; and in return introduced the Latin
rite, something like the rule of St. Benedict, and above
all, the now Canonical Easter, kept on the Lord's Day.

The result of these changes was a great vital activity
and enthusiasm. A new missionary spirit informed the
place and the sons of St. Mary went out not only to
many places in England, founding religious houses and
filling sees, but they have some of the honour of the
missions to Germany in the VIII Century. Wilfred of
Crediton studied here. Relics of St. Willibrord were
treasured as pertaining to the house, and Bega the
Abbess, one of the benefactors, is perhaps one of the
holy women who helped these missionaries in person.

After Ine, king succeeded king, but beyond the confirmation of privileges and grants there is little of interest
to record. Wessex, from its Somerton centre, was
struggling with Mercia : but in 800 the great Egbert
came to the throne, who united the South in one large

[1] 10 acres are a fardel, 40 a virgate, 160 a hide, and 640 a fief.

kingdom. It was in his reign that the Danes first appeared, and Glastonbury was once more in perils from the heathen. In 846 the armies of Somerset and Dorset met and slaughtered the robbers at the mouth of the Parrett in a victory which freed the coast for a genera-tion. The men of war and the men of prayer must both have put forth all their energies here ; but the red tide of battle and plunder was always getting nearer to the holy spot, until in 878 the robbers were completely masters of the land. Then King Alfred was watching from the fastness of Athelney the tide which he could not stem, and not watching Denewulf's cakes. Was it the very meanness of the old church which saved it, when the land was forsaken of her chief men ? The lowly building and poor estate were, perhaps, not tempting to the incendiaries. But more probably still the Danes were touched by some feeling of awe for so holy a spot, such as all heathenish persons have not felt. Never-theless Cenwald two centuries before, though still a heathen, had granted to the Abbey two hides of land. In spite of all the danger, as we know, the old church still escaped Alfred's three successive battles, which swept the Danes out of Wessex, Pen, Aglea and Edington, were, almost certainly, fought at Pen, Edgarley, and the Somer-set Edington The routed robbers fled to their base at Downend, a loop of the Parrett near Dunball Station : hence came the christening of Guthrum at Aller and his chrisom-loosing at Wedmore, and the peace there. King Alfred not only renewed the Charters, but gave presents to the monastery, among them being a piece of the true Cross which Pope Marinus had sent to him. His

successors had the same enthusiasm. Ethelstan brought
relics of two Saxon saints and the bones of Pope Urban,
that honest martyr-bishop of the III Century, who
gave the Ember days to the Church's year. Edmund
the elder sent from the North the unwithered arm of
St. Oswald, with relics of Aidan, Bede, Hilda, and
Benedict Biscop. The endowment of the place in this
way is remarkable. It became a custom for kings to
furnish it with relics. A piece of Isaiah's tomb, a fragment of the Temple floor, even some hairs of our Lord,
bits of the sponges, of the column of scourging, one
thorn from His crown, a thread of Our Lady's robe,
two bones of the holy Baptist, relics of all the Apostles,
of the Evangelists, of all the black-letter Saints in our
present calendar, St. Hugh's hair shirt, many things
of SS. Thomas and Edmund of Canterbury and of
numerous others—virgins, martyrs, doctors, and confessors—were accumulated. A passionate desire for
memorials of the masters of the holy life seems perverse
to those who prefer the earthly wealth which was spent
for centuries to gain these treasures; but surely the
wish to have one thread of the robe of scorn or one
crumb of those barley loaves follows naturally from a
simple love of Christ? And who that honours the noble
and great who are gone would not wish to have something, say, of St. Martin or St. Ambrose? To say that
the monks were too little critical is another matter. A
great love and much serving is generally open to that
charge.

The year A.D. 936 is an important one, for in it the
man " who was for thirty years the mainstay of the

safety and glory of the English," the great St. Dunstan, was made Abbot by his friend, King Edmund the Elder. Both the source and the inspiration of Dunstan's life was Glastonbury. Here he was born and educated. Here he learned from the Irish scholars, music, painting, and metal work ; and from the witness of this Church, to dream of and to build up a better country. He was nominated to the post when very young and became by Edmund's Charter practically king of the XII Hides.

He had seen the great Ethelstan buried under the altar, with relics brought from Brittany, with gold and silver gifts ; but he found the buildings decayed, the discipline uncertain, and the educational work disorganised. Here, where he had coped with the devil of lust by the more

S. Dunstan.
Bodleian Library Window.

absorbing delight of metal work,[1] he fought with other devils of disorder and savagery, and built, from plans brought from Normandy, the more regular Benedictine Monastery, which was to become so powerful an influence on English life. Possibly those plans

[1] He was making a chalice, when he routed the devil with his stithy tongs.

came from Duke Richard's new foundation at Mont
S. Michel ; but nothing of his outward building now
remains, nor has the place anything of his painting and
other craft ; but he made the monastery a storehouse
of learning and a home of the arts, which did not perish
when his little cell (5 ft. by 2½ ft.) was burnt, with his
workshop and edifices. Before Edmund was murdered
in A.D. 943 the Benedictine rule was finally and formally
established. This was, in short, something of a constitu-
tional monarchy, with common table, common property,
assigned duties, cleanness, labour, learning, and great
hospitality. The high standard of zeal and strenuous-
ness so delighted Edred that he made the place his
treasury, and large presents were brought to the church
and school. He wished to make all religious houses
of this austere and useful type, for the secular clergy
with their wives and goods were then in an unworthy
state. The reaction under Edwy was severe, but it was
a worldly and unbottomed reaction. Dunstan was
banished, but his work was too enduring for any success-
ful reaction. The short, fierce, warlike Edgar more
than restored it. He confirmed the privileges, divided
his gold and ivory sceptre in two, laid it on the altar,
and took back but half of it, as a parable of his views of
Church and State. He enlisted the Pope's sympathy.
The sons of the old Church went out to build and govern.
Abingdon, Ely, Peterborough, Thorney, Winchester,
Worcester, and many other places felt their influence.
Peace, order and justice returned to a well-governed
land. Edgar was " the Romulus, Cyrus, Alexander,
and Charlemagne of England," who, in spite of some

strange tales of love and fury, held up Christ's head ;
and was thought by the scholar Abbot most worthy to
have the capitular chapel of the great minster. Edgar
died in A.D. 975 and (like Edmund and Ethelstan) was
buried here, but in the XI Century his body was translated into a reliquary he had himself given for other
relics.

The very year that Dunstan died, 988, the horrors
of the third Danish war began with the pillage of
Watchet. [1] Battles were won and lost. The fleets
were bought off and returned. Dorset was ravaged,
Hampshire, Sussex, Kent, and the churches burnt.
Treachery attempted what arms could not do. The
massacres were avenged. Archbishop Alphege, son of
Glastonbury, died magnificently for the poor. At last
Swegen over-ran Wessex, and not only the Mother of
Saints but all England was at his feet. Yet no torch
was put to the old church. This is so great a miracle that
at least one modern writer, thinking Swegen grievously
remiss in his incendiary duties, has made him burn out
the church, contrary to the opinion of Cnut, who found
·it standing shortly afterwards. The old tale is that
they came to the gate " Hawete," a mile from the church.

[1] It is during this war that the monks claim to have found
at Canterbury, recognised by a ring and translated to
Glastonbury (1012), the relics of their most beloved Father
Dunstan. Even if their claim be disallowed, there is no reason
to write them down knaves and forgers. There were many
graves at Canterbury. They may, in hurry, confusion, and
twilight, and in the fear of the Danes, have opened the wrong
one in the deserted church ; but they heard the Abbey bells
ring, without hands, a peal of welcome, and until Warham's
time the dispute was not determined.

Most of the robbers, hearing of its guard of saints, retired in awe, but some mockers pressed on. Then the

S. Alphege.
From Sculpture, Wells Cathedral

Virgin Mother struck them with blindness, which after they had repented, was taken from them, so that they gave a cross of gold and jewels, in memory of their double deliverance. After this came the days of Cnut and his great opponent, Edmund of the Ironsides. The first of the five great fights was at Pen Selwood (in 1016) in Somerset, and when Edmund died, his last wish was to be numbered with the saints at the ancient place, as indeed he was,[1] and Cnut came here in person, prayed at the tomb, gave a charter of confirmation, and presented a sheeny pall, inwoven with peacock harles fixing his seal in the wooden church in 1022, that is, five years after he was King of England. Even Harthacnut gave a shrine for St. Benignus. But the Abbots under Edward and Harold wasted the goods

[1] The muster for Pen fight possibly was made on Edmund's Hill.

of the Abbey, and the success of half a century was worse than fear and war to the monastery. Yet what a record there is ! Before the Conquest nine Primates were given to England,[1] and bishops numberless. The place was the embodiment of English religion, with its uncodified laws, uncollated customs, laxity of formal discipline, insistent customs, and carelessness about possible future evils, some of which had already beset it. Consequently neither William the Conqueror and settler, nor the severe, rather legal Lanfranc could be expected to look upon it with the eyes of " *incomparabilis Edgarus*," or of its English lovers.

AFTER THE CONQUEST

IT is hardly wonderful that William I and Lanfranc dealt harshly with " the second Rome," which was above all diocesan and much civil control. The Conqueror seized several manours, Montacute, Tintinhull, and others, impoverished the Abbey and took Abbot Ailnoth into his train, as half-prisoner, half-courtier. Any share which the Abbey took in the last revolt of the West and the siege of Montacute Castle was, perhaps, never known ; but the Council inspected the charters and gave a somewhat ungracious confirmation of what remained. In 1077, the inevitable Norman Abbot,

[1] Bertwald, Athelm, St. Dunstan, Ethelgar, Sigeric, Alfric, St. Alphege, Living and Ethelnoth.

Turstin, came, and the first attempt was made to subdue the Abbey to the See, but was resisted. The conflict of race and thought broke out over a trivial matter. Turstin resolved to bring in the Roman rite and to discard "the Gregorian music and office" for the Latin plain song and use. The monks rebelled. Armed men were brought into the church and blood was spilt. Two monks were slain at the altar and fourteen wounded. So great a scandal caused William to order Turstin back to Normandy, and to pacify the indignant English by grants of land to Our Lady of Glastonbury. William Rufus, for a bribe of £500, restored this Turstin, who, grown wiser, translated the relics of St. Benignus to the high altar of the Eastern Church. A monk from Caen

could not but build, at this heyday of Norman architecture, and there was a new stone church erected to the East of St. Dunstan's, but his building, not being worthy of the Abbey, was carefully levelled by his successor, Herlwin—an act reformatory not deformatory, for the stones and mouldings would be kept and used again. Perhaps we have in the arch over the holy well the sole remains of the Conqueror's fiery Abbot. Herlwin, also a monk of Caen, succeeded in 1101, and ruled for 19 years. Though he had been looked upon as a near housekeeper, he astonished the brothers by his

S. Hugh.
From S. Mary's Tower, Oxford.

The Galilee (Interior).

See pages 27-31.

The Galilee from the S.W.

See pages 27–31.

generous public spirit. " Let us do what we can, if we cannot do what we would," were his marching orders, from Terence. He began a grander church, perhaps with Western towers, enlarged the monastery, increased the revenues, and threatened to clip the porter's ears if he refused admission to the poor. He also procured a splendid crucifix and died the year that Prince William was drowned, A.D. 1120. His successor, Sigfried, brother to the merry Ralph of Canterbury and also from Say, was one of Lanfranc's disciples. Except that he supported Anselm in the Investiture quarrel, he had made no particular mark when he left for Chichester, being a gentle, unbusinesslike man. Then came the learned Henry of Blois, nephew to Henry I, who afterwards filled so large a part in political history by securing the crown for his brother Stephen. He found the buildings dilapidated and the revenues in confusion, but flung himself boldly into the work of reconstruction. A royal palace called the Castle arose, a chapter house, cloyster, lavatory, refectory, dormitory, infirmary, chapel, a great stone gateway, and a large bell-tower. He discovered the super altar of St. David with its great sapphire, which was securely hidden from furtive eyes. He stored the library with books—Pliny, Origen Jerome, Anselm and others. When he moved to Winchester, he still ruled by sub-abbots. He enlisted the help of three Popes, of three Kings, and even of the Empress Maud. He had a light set perpetually before the altar of the old church, which perhaps was less wise than pious. When he died, in 1171, the Abbey was strong, full, and prosperous, and had struck its roots even into newly-conquered

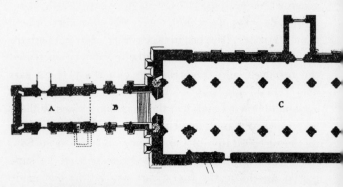

A. St. Mary's Church.
B. The Galilee.
C. Nave of SS. Peter and Paul.
D. Central Spire showing Stone Screen (1322).
E. Choir, containing tombs of Edmunds, Elder and Ironsides
    and King Arthur.

Ireland. The monks were, perhaps, more in
number now than before or since, for Innocent III
limited them to 60, and that number was never afterwards exceeded. Henry's zeal collected the many
memorials of the newly-martyred St. Thomas, to
whom his successor also (Robert of Winchester) was
devoted in person and in cause. These men struck the
note very strongly of adhesion to the Pope against kings
and bishops, which was so significant in after times.
Robert, too, was a builder. His chapel and chamber
alone of all the buildings, with Henry's bell-tower,
escaped the great fire.

In 1178 the Abbacy was vacant, and Henry II, glad
to have command of its revenues in his wars with France

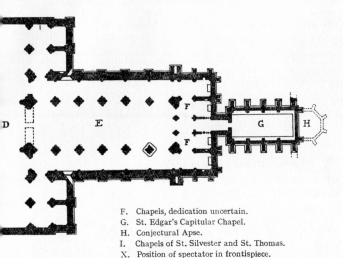

F. Chapels, dedication uncertain.
G. St. Edgar's Capitular Chapel.
H. Conjectural Apse.
I. Chapels of St. Silvester and St. Thomas.
X. Position of spectator in frontispiece.

and his own family, kept it vacant, and appointed one
Peter de Marcy to take charge of it. This wily Clug-
niac Chamberlain tried, by some liberality and more
promises, to win the monks to elect himself. But he
was a worldly, rapacious priest, who had borne arms
and killed his man ; so they hung back. In 1183, on
Christmas Eve, he pretended to say Mass in the wooden
church and was detected profaning the mysteries
Instead of exposing him and re-dedicating the church,
the monks concealed the impiety ; but on 25th May,
1184, on the feast of that Pope Urban, whose body lay
there, a fearful fire arose. It burnt to ashes, not only
the splendid Norman Church and monastery, but the
ancient House of God, with all the historic accumulations

of art, learning and piety. A wild cry of horror and consternation arose through the country. The poor old troubled king, not without some spur of conscience, hastened to the rescue. He sent his Chamberlain, Ralph Fitz-Stephen, a man of honour, talent and devoutness, to rebuild and uphold the shattered House. Ralph first fed the poor monks who were huddled in the scanty remains of their monastery and then " in the very spot where the ancient church had first stood, with loveliest work and moulded stone, he completed the Church of St. Mary, and spared nothing in adorning it. He repaired all the houses, and finally laid the foundation of the loveliest church, and enlarged it to a length of 400 feet, with a breadth of 80 feet. He pressed forward the work, and spared no expense. What could not be got from Glastonbury the royal bounty supplied. The stones laid in the foundation of this church were both those of the great palace of Henry, and those of the whole wall which surrounded the abbey. Thus he erected a great part of the church, and would have finished the same in rare style, if the Lord had not taken away the life of the king." The saintly relics, salvaged from the fire, were the bodies of SS. Patrick, Indractus, and his companions, Gildas the historian, and some of the relics of ' St. Dunstan,' too. These were collected in shrines, as also were the shoulder and arm of St. Oswald.

St. Mary's Chapel.
See page 27.

The North Door of St. Joseph's Chapel of Our Lady.
See page 28.

ST. MARY'S CHAPEL AND THE GALILEE

THE interest of Glastonbury now shifts from its chronicles to its actual stones, but before examining them, let us bear in mind that in these last days of Henry II, two builders were at work, whose records in stone and chronicle shed light upon these works of Ralph, son of Stephen. The first is bishop Reginald Fitz-Jocelin, of Wells, whose work in the three Western arches of that Choir, and the four Eastern bays of the Nave, is improved or transition Norman, and whose still earlier exquisite North Porch was erected by the same school of Somerset masons as wrought the lovely work of this chapel of St. Mary. The second great builder was St. Hugh, of Avalon and Lincoln, whose early English work in his Cathedral is closely followed in the Galilee, the great porch now united to St. Mary's. This resemblance alone would suggest that St. Hugh's Somerset masons, who built Witham also, came to Lincoln, and returned home to build the work here. But as St. Mary's also resembles the work of St. Hugh's own Avalon, particularly in the doors, and we add to this St. Hugh's passionate devotion to relics, it becomes almost certain that we have in these Glastonbury stones some of the thoughts of the loveliest of our Saints, as well as the work of the most interesting of our kings.

The East end of the great church, that is up to the fourth severy from the central arch, was begun at this

E

time, and some modern authorities say that both buildings were meant to be detached, but that is not to be gathered from ancient writers. St. Mary's Chapel was bounded by four lovely turrets, of which only two remain, and at first had no crypt. As a tribute to its venerable site, it was built in a somewhat archaic style, and the position of the doors and four windows doubtless represent the doors and windows of the ancient church. Those doors are themselves worthy of careful study. The stone is the enduring Doulting stone, carefully squared and fitted with rich chevron mouldings round the arcade, and the Norman zig-zag moulding round the windows. There is no possible reason why this place should not be restored to some of its original completeness and purpose, roofed, floored, and glazed, and preserved for future generations ; even though we grudge the glory of the paintings, which once lit up its walls, and spare the golden super-altar with its great sapphire, and do not either produce or detect such saints as once rested under every foot of its stone and leaden pavement. St. Joseph's well, before the crypt was made, used to be outside the walls, and supplied the water for the holy sacrifice, the lavabo asperges, and ablutions. It is said to have been fed from Chalice well.

The doors are not only interesting as a marvel of delicate design in stone leaf-work, but the unfinished *fascia* on the South tells the tale of how, when harassed old King Henry died, his swash-buckling son left the work undone, for the excitements of the Crusade. It tells, too, how the builders of 1184-9 carved the stones when these were in position. The doors each had a tympanum, possibly of stone lace-work, stretched behind the arch. Those of Avalon in Burgundy have sculptures in front of this. The design of the carving seems to have been to tell the tale of Nature and Grace, the *Eva* and *Ave* epitomizing man's life. On the South is the creation of woman, and the earliest wedding day, but the artist ended here, for the royal revenues and those of the Abbey too, were diverted to the war with Saladin. The north door has puzzled many students, and been food for guesses more assured than happy. The lowest *fascia* tells the tale of Our Lady. The Angel appears to Anna, who meets her husband Joachim. The holy Virgin is born, and dedicated in the Temple which stands behind the chamber. The central panel is the Annunciation, and then nothing is quite plain until the Mother of God is seated, crowned at the last. The eighteen ovals in the third *fascia* may contain the story of the Epiphany, the King riding to Jerusalem, being warned in separate beds, Herod with his Knights, the Murder of the Innocents, and in the last a pilgrim, St. Joseph of Arimathæa, setting forth. These keys are unsatisfactory, and the work is dirty, decayed, and mutilated. If these are the three kings, where is the adoration ? and why is one of them like a woman ? If we turn for aid to the Gospels of Mary and the Innocency, we get little help. The leprous woman, healed by the Saviour's bath water, the sick princess and her husband, suggest themselves ; but none of the Apocryphal or Scripture stories seem to fit the carvings. The explanations all halt, and it is better to admit defeat rather than to advance uncatholic explanations, which have no power to explain. The carvings on the tympanum might explain it all, if we had them.

When Henry II died, the monks bestirred themselves to get an Abbot, and Richard being anxious for money, the way was open. They remembered the great Henry de Blois, and chose another Henry, also of royal blood, called De Soliaco, of Sully or Swansea. He had been a friend to the late king, and was intimate with Richard. One of the first things he did was to search for the grave of King Arthur, about whom the late king had been interested when he heard the story from the Welsh bards. There were close to the North-west turret two pyramid pillars, one of five stories, 28 feet high, and one of four, and 26 feet high. The loftier contained the names of fifteen persons, and the latter of four Among these were Kentwin of Northumbria, Wilfrid of York, Earnfled, and others. On the South side, facing the second window, were two grooved crosses of great antiquity,[1] and between these last, tradition said the king and his queen were buried. Abbot Henry dug deep, and almost despaired, when at the depth of seven feet, they found a leaden cross with " Here lies King Arthur, the renowned king in the isle of Avalon," in Latin. On digging as much lower, they found a dugout oak coffin, with the bones of a very tall man, with many wounds in his skull, and the queen with golden hair delicately braided, which fell to dust at a touch. The remains of both were buried in the Abbey Church. The foolish theory that this was monkish imposture is

[1] 608 years, says John, c. A.D. 1400.

confuted by the dates, for the search was set on foot
by Henry II, the discovery made in the reign of Richard,
who preferred the bones of one marching soldier, before
the resting ones of all dead kings.

The Galilee to the East of St. Mary's Chapel was,
we may conclude, finished under De Soliaco (1189–93)
and more by the monks than by their chief. But we
must bear in mind that Abbot Henry's later actions
raised a storm against his memory, so that Adam de
Domerham would be likely to grudge rather than pay
him his deserts. Attention, revenue, and zeal were
after Henry's day swallowed up in the political stress of
Richard's later years, and still more by the great quarrel
with the Abbot Bishop Savaric ; so that we shall hardly
do wrong in concluding that this splendid porch was
finished in the years mentioned. It has been altered
and adapted, but was in the new Early English style,
with three pointed windows on each side, below which
was an arcade of trefoil arches, comparable with Lincoln
and Cleeve. It seems to have been built by the same
masons as those who raised Our Lady's Church, but
was divided from it. The marks of a great staircase,
leading up to the West door of the Abbey Church may
be noticed. The crypt belongs to the XV Century,
being made to allow of burials within the hallowed
precincts, and was then built of old Norman stones, in
the perpendicular style.[1] When the crypt was made,
the Galilee was taken into the Lady Chapel, the West

---

[1] The coarse thwart masonry, which keeps the walls of the
Lady Chapel from collapse, was placed there by the clumsy piety
of 1826.

door of the great church being blocked by the reredos, screen, and Lady altar, which projected 7 feet from the disused door.

THE MONKS

Bellcote of St. Margaret's
Almshouse Chapel.

BEFORE we pass on to the evil days of Savaric, it is interesting to ask what these monks were like. The Abbot had now obtained the mitre from Pope Cælestine III, and wore the ring, gloves, sandals, dalmatic and tunic on great occasions. The monks wore habitually dark cowls or sleeveless hooded outer garments.

Each had two of these, with two frocks or cassocks, two woven vests, two pairs of linen breeches, four pairs of long hose, and every year a new pelisse of black wool. He had a new pair of thick shoes once a year, and for winter night shoes, two coverlets to his bed and ten pairs of short hose. He fed upon measured portions of bread, meat, fish, biscuits, mead, beer and wine,

according to the dignity of the feasts, in three meals
and two snacks, or two meals and three snacks. There
were 58 professed brothers, of whom the majority—
say 35—were priests. Nearly all were natives not only
of England but of Somerset, and Glastonbury was
always decidedly Wessex. For this reason it may
have been less urbane, but it was the more beloved by
its neighbours than, for instance, were the Abbies of
St. Alban or St. Edmund. The new honours to the
Abbot, given in the unhappy year 1191, enabled him
to do some of the work of a bishop, such as consecrating
vestments, and gave him some of the look of a bishop,
too ; so that there were both hopes and fears that the
place might become a see. Bishop Reginald of Bath
died soon after and bequeathed his jealous fears, and
contrived to bequeath his see also, to his kinsman
Savaric.

THE BISHOP ABBOTS

SAVARIC is the type of a Churchman not uncommon
at this time. Of high lineage, a relative of the
Emperor Henry VI, a dashing sportsman, of extravagant
habits, a man of courts and travel, he accomplished that
divorce of salary from duty, at which the cynic says we
are all aiming. He was King Richard's intermediary
with the Emperour, and being by favour advanced to the
See of Bath, he persuaded his kinsman and his king that
the diocese would be better served if he were both Abbot

and Bishop in one. Henry de Soliaco was promoted to
the See of Winchester, the king accepted Bath, and
Savaric became the angel of the Church of Wells and
Glastonbury. He also became Chancellor of Burgundy. [1]
He got back to his ecclesiastical duties only in 1197.
He was a man of intelligence and had set himself to
solve a grave question, the relation of the monastic
houses to the Episcopal government, that is to the
common life of the Church. Bishop Reginald had tried
the simple solution of bringing the Abbot into the chapter,
where his own headship was promptly contested. At
bottom this question is a still further one. Is the Church
an absolute monarchy under the Pope, or is she a con-
stitutional and decentralized government under bishops,
though federated and united perhaps under one Head ?
The monastic claim to be extra diocesan, when the
monasteries were powerful must have thrown the sees
out of gear. In the final event it always was and will
be to the interest of Papal power to support monks
against bishops, but the whole existence of these splendid
monuments of faith, art and learning—the Monasteries
—was imperilled by the very victories they obtained
over the common local life of the Church. The bitterness, arrogance and unreasonableness of both sides
the wearisome debates about trivial or worldly matters,
the vices, or the very virtues of the combatants, confuse
the issues. The broad fact is this, that the great and
glorious House of Glastonbury, for three centuries, was
opposed to the idea of the government of the bishop
and pastor of the Church in Somerset, and constantly

[1] Said to be an honorary post, but no doubt with perquisites.

appealed both to Pope and King against that government. Thus the Abbey chose the crowns and thrones that vanish rather than the foundation which was from the beginning. Neither its loveliness nor its most venerable story, nor its associations of blessedness nor its deep educational value, could save it from the shameful fate which awaits all things not upon this foundation.

Bishop Savaric came to his Abbey in mighty state with a train of soldiers, burst in the doors, preized open the presses, prankt the secular canons in the holy vestments and enthroned himself, with the help of " eight traitors " among the monks. The murmurers were chased with swords and sticks from the church, locked in the farmory and kept without food or without drink on alternate days. Literal and spiritual weapons prevailed, and they submitted. The gallant medical novice, William Pike, who had headed a deputation to the Pope and been elected anti-abbot, was excommunicated. His use of the great seal was repudiated before the merchants. In vain he dashed off again to Rome, for Savaric's arm was there before him, and he died so very conveniently that the brethren were assured he had been poisoned. Until the death of Savaric in A.D. 1205 it may be concluded that the building of the great church of SS. Peter and Paul stood still ; the discipline, hospitality, and order were weightily diminished and the worship much neglected. Then the king, bishop, nobles of England, and Innocent III also, made up their minds to abate the scandal and restore the ancient status by dividing the see and Abbey, but the troubles of King John's reign and the vigour of bishop-abbot Jocelin put off the final partition until 1216. Jocelin was not only a great builder, but he lived under the compelling power of much criticism. Though it is not admitted by the chronicler, who merely tells us that the monks were pinched in necessaries, the great church must have begun again to be built. Literary, scholastic, and other work went on. Fifteen books were transcribed for the library. [1]

ABBOTS NOT BISHOPS

IN 1219, when England was so badly governed by Pandulf the legate, Jocelin affixed his seal to a deed which released the abbey from episcopal sway : but he first docked it of considerable sources of revenue, eft it shorn of some of its insignia, and thus handed it over to William Vigor, a staunch opponent of the bishop's power. This man immediately increased the monies paid to the master of the works, and so sped forward the buildings ; but after five years, the Church was not ready, and the Abbot, at his death, had to be buried in the Chapter House. Robert, Prior of Bath, succeeded him, a gentle and pious man ; but the English policy of De Burgh and Stephen Langton is plainly seen in the Royal decrees, which grant concession after

[1] Noted Psalter, Decreta, Radulphus on Leviticus, Notes and text of Genesis and Exodus, Two Volumes of Pauline Epistles, SS. Matthew and Mark, SS. Luke and John, with Notes, Deuteronomy and Comment, a Versed Bible, Joshua and Judges, Two Missals and Hamo.

concession to bishop Jocelin, the patronage of the Abbey, disafforestations, advowsons, and court rights, all of which were intended to check the idea of a state within a state. That policy, therefore, was not beloved at Glastonbury.

In 1235, a new abbot, Michael de Amesbury, was consecrated in London by Jocelin and took the command of a foundation "hugely wounded." He was neither saint nor scholar, but after a youth of travel and adventure, had become a keen, shrewd, vigorous man of affairs. His loyalty to the king, when Churchmen mostly stood for Simon de Montford, gave him great power at Court, a power he used to wrest back most of the concessions. He surpassed all his forerunners in building. Almost all parts of the domain felt his hand. A hundred dwellings rose. Innumerable advantages were gained or recovered. The Pope smiled once more. The great church, now roofed in, rang with the music of the Mass, and the major altar could be used, and was supplied with a service of silver. A grand processional cross of silver, a shrine of "St. Dunstan's" head, and other splendours, tell of active worship now possible, and even the Tor Church, dedicated to the Abbot's patron, felt the benefits of so able a ruler. When Michael died, old and blind in 1253, he was the first man to be buried in the new church, and his grave lay before the Altar of St. Thomas, in the North Transept. So strong did the jubilant monks now feel, that they boldly fixed an epitaph to proclaim that Michael had broken the deceits of the serpent, and their own chains.[1]

[1] To the See.

That was his triumph : but he also found the house
bare and left it solvent, with 800 head of cattle, 6,000
sheep, 300 swine, and a year's corn in its granaries.
For the next nine years, Roger Forde, a literary man,
succeeded the man of business. He talked eloquently,
wrote finely, contended sharply, and did nothing. He
found the bishop as hot-headed and controversial as
himself. Perhaps his tongue got him even into worse
trouble, for he was killed in a brawl at Bromley. Tall
Robert of Petherton, another son of the House (1261–74),
had enough to do to nurse the revenues in the civil
wars, without any forward movement. His were the days
of Lewes and Evesham, with the struggle to enforce the
great Charter. As we should expect from what has gone
before, Glastonbury had no sympathy with the baronial
party, but supported the cause of Prince Edward. When
Robert died of consumption in 1274, there was an un-
seemly struggle with the bishop's men over the funeral ;
but the monks prevailed, and they buried him next to
Abbot Michael in the North Transept. John of Taunton,
also a brother of the Abbey, was his successor. John
was neither a mere scholar, a mere lawyer, nor a mere
man of business, but alert and alive to both worlds,
the visible and invisible. He appealed to the old friend
of the House, now Edward I. It was a golden moment.
Not only was this umpire of an exalted and just build,
but his chancellor, Robert Brunell, was now bishop
of Bath and Wells. The result was a characteristic
and legal " final concord," in which the rights of both
parties were defined. This gave a time of peace much
needed, for in 1275 an earthquake levelled the old

Church of St. Michael on the Tor, and did other damage.
But John de Taunton profited by peace, and extended
the domain on all sides, not least by acquiring Bechary,
now a ruined chapel, but a rich soiled island ; and
Doulting, the quarrying place of stone. He needed
the latter, for he built much—granges, chambers,
dovecots, and a new gate of Glastonbury, perhaps
on the Wells road. He also rebuilt Bechary and Godney
Chapels. He gathered together a fine library of Com-
mentators, which were lodged, if a chance phrase is
in its right place, in the Galilee, [1] together with Albertus
Magnus, Augustine, many works of the new doctor
Aquinas, Peter Mauricius, works on natural history
and perspective drawing, with Kilwardby on the Sen-
tences—perhaps this last was given by the author.
The Aristotelian nominalism, that child of Arabia
and the Crusades, found favour in the Abbey, rather
than the realism which was taught by the Sons of
St. Francis. Kilwardby himself, the Friar Archbishop,
was of course a realist and possibly gave his book as
a slight corrective to the library.

In 1278, during Holy Week, Edward I, the greatest
of our kings, came to Glastonbury, with Queen Eleanor,
and a great train. They were met on the West Pennard
road by a grand procession. Next day they were joined
by the Archbishop, who was welcomed in the same way :
for he came, by request to consecrate oils, and to ordain.
The former act was the cause of an unpleasant dispute
between secular canons and monks, courteously settled
by Kilwardby in favour of his hosts. Three king's

[1] Domerham, 574.

men were ordained priests—at the request of the Abbot
—and the Archbishop was allowed to sing the High
Mass at Easter. Next day the king wanted to hold his
Assize here, but it was explained to him that he would
thereby infringe the liberties, which he said he would
rather enlarge ; and he thus transferred the Assize to
Street.   That same night was another significant incident.   Philip de Cogan, a servant of the Abbey, had
a brawl with one of the Mazseurs, or royal bodyguard,
and drew a knife upon his man.   He was arrested for
high treason, but instantly liberated by the Abbot,
whose bailiffs then made amends for the fault of Philip.
The moral of the drama is quite plain.

Next day the Court and Convent assembled and
saw the opening of King Arthur's new tomb, for the
translation of his bones.   A stately mausoleum had
been prepared behind the High Altar, and thither King
Edward bore the king's bones, and his queen carried
Guinevere's wonderfully beautiful remains, wrapped in
precious palls.   There they were sealed by the royal
signets, but the skulls[1] were left outside for greater
devotion.   Thus Edward proclaimed to the Welsh his
care and love for their great leader, in the part he was
preparing to play, and perhaps claimed the fulfilment
of the prophecy of *rex futurus* for himself.

Every care was taken, even to the inspection of
victuals, to give precedence to the Abbey men, and
thus the visit was a great triumph for those very principles which ended in the destruction of the monastery.
In the meantime the cost of lavish hospitality, a number

[1] Arthur's with ten wounds.

of heavy law suits, and the taxation of the clergy, clogged the enterprise of the abbot and made him deal hardly with his tenants, so that he incurred their wrath and was unable to continue the buildings, as he wished. But he managed to establish a thing which had been long sought for, by obtaining a declaration that he was a tenant *in capite*, holding direct from the Crown, and this both saved irksome dealings with the bishop and secured the abbot a seat in Parliament as a spiritual lord. John de Taunton died in 1290, catching his death at the funeral of the queen mother. He was buried in the South side of the North Transept, and over him was placed an epitaph, which called him one who had spent much, worked much, and taught Christ's lore. The chancellor-bishop died soon after him. The end of the wonderful XIII Century saw an outburst of rich ritual and splendid art work. We hear of a cross of crystal, a baldichino woven with leopards and birds in gold, an Indian red cope with castles and lions and its morse of hammered silver, tunics of silk and samite braided with the Arms of England, and much else of magnificence. John of Kent, the next abbot, was equally an artist, and erected a great rood with a crucifix and SS. Mary and John, procuring glorious vestments besides, and an aspersory of silver and ivory with splendid jewelry. He freed the house from a Lucca merchant to whom it was in debt, and carried forward the great church, so that it was ready when he died for the solemn consecration. This was performed under Geoffry Fromont in 1303, while Edward I, in defiance of the Pope, was assaulting

Scotland. Abbot Geoffrey began the great hall and
the chapter house and was a man of fine tastes like his
predecessors. We hear of wonderful copes, velvet grey,
with moon and stars, red satin picked out with parrots,
and of six woven carpets, a refinement learnt in the
Crusades, some of them green or golden with parrots
and roses, and much else ; all of which must have made
the great church to glitter with rich colouring. Even
Walter de Taunton, though abbot only for a few days,
left a stone screen in front of the choir, curiously carved
with ten statues ; another rood and ten copes bordered
with feather work and elaborate pictures of saints,
scallops, leopards, ladders and griffins. A greater crafts-
man still was Abbot Adam de Sodbury (1322-35), whose
zeal upheld worthily the tradition of St. Dunstan. He
vaulted in stone the greater part of the Church of
SS. Peter and Paul, painted the walls with kings, heroes,
saints and benefactors, enriched the altars with curious
works of silver and stone, made the chapels of St.
Silvester, the Pope who baptised Constantine, and of
St. George, of whom the Abbey possessed a bone. He
cast and hung in the great tower six bells, no doubt of
the conical shape of the period, and five more, which
he hung in the bell-tower, of which the site is now unknown.[1] It is uncertain whether any of these bells
survived through two centuries, but in 1544 there were
eight very great bells in the tower and three most huge
" in the churchyard," and in Edward VI's reign 100 lbs.
of bell metal was still " in the chauntrie." Bells and

[1] Was it to the South of St. Mary's Chapel, where there is still
some ruined masonry ?

The Galilee Porch.
See page 31.

The Abbot's Kitchen.

bell-ringing were among the traditions of Glastonbury. For miles around the villages must have heard their missionary sound, have learnt the days and hours by their resonant melodies, and felt the tragedy of their silenced voices. Abbot Adam it was who caused Peter Lightfoot, one of his monks, to construct the great clock, which was formerly in the South Transept and was since lodged in the North Transept of Wells Cathedral. This was not actually the first clock, but was the first clock in a modern sense, not only in England but in Europe. In 1298 Paul's Jacks were set up in London and struck bells at regular intervals, without a dial, other than the sundial. In 1326 a mechanical Planetarium, called a horologe, was erected in St. Alban's Abbey. But Brother Peter combined both principles, and provided a regular escapement for equable motion and three dial circles. The twenty-four hours are marked by a revolving star, the minutes by a smaller star, and the age of the moon is shown on the inmost circle. The old iron works are still to be seen, with an added pendulum, at South Kensington. It is still a witness to the rare mechanical intelligence, which the Benedictine order fostered, to the great benefit of later contrivers. It is interesting to note that patronage of this art survived even to the last abbot, whose watch is in existence and has been often pictured. This is of the earlier type, which Jeremia Metzger was making at Augsburg, before the bow for hanging it had been introduced and watches were worn with seals in the girdle. Of the other works of art, jewelry, chalices, suits of vestments broidered with beasts, silver butterflies,

View through Choir, looking South.

purple birds and what not, there is a long list, as also of his illuminated Bible, school Histories, "Properties of things," Acts of saints, precious Psalters, and a Benedictionary. The scriptorium was no sinecure, and the workshops were kept busy, as were the voices and hands of all the monks in works or offices for the living and the dead.

It is pleasant to dwell on these things, for the other glimpses we get into the history show constant feuds with the bishop, full of unhappy incident and mutual discourtesy. For instance, when John XXII imposed a tax of a tenth, the abbot was unable to enforce payment, and Edward II had to quicken the bishop to come to his aid. Still earlier, when the bishop (1312) made his visitation he found, both here and at Bath, a combination to defeat him by oaths of secrecy. Constant law-suits about land crop up, monks and retainers destroy See property, and the bishop invades the Abbey possessions, to publish fulminations against spiteful persons officially unknown. But the work of study, invention, education, and worship is a noiseless one and goes with small chronicle. A large community with many servants, from liveried squires to keepers and woodmen, with land in many parishes, and several counties, could hardly escape some unpleasant details. If we could judge fairly, this Abbey would probably compare well with lay-lords in this troublesome time and certainly very well with other great houses.

While on the one hand party strife ran so high that even Dean Godilee of Wells was accused of firing the moor to windward with intent to burn out the Abbey, it is pleasant to remember that Glastonbury shows a whole-hearted enthusiasm for dignity of worship and without pause or lapse, for the cause of learning. If the Franciscan movement found no favour here, neither can we find boisterous plays performed in the great Church, such as disgraced the Cathedral at Wells ; nor was there any huckstering in the House of God. If we examine the twenty-three livings of which the Abbey held the advowson, we find they were served by incumbents of great weight. Take West Monckton, for instance. Out of nineteen nominations, ten were of men honoured by Church or State in various ways. One became President of Magdalen, two were afterwards Archdeacons and others were men of note. Even outlying parishes were served by priests whose names meet us in the annals of Oxford. The pupils of Glastonbury made their mark at the University, and Glastonbury benefactions helped to build and embellish even St. Mary's Church.[1] The library so resolutely accumulated impressed scholars as the best in England, and its cruel destruction has lost us several links in the national history. Before the middle of the XIII Century it

[1] Wood. R. FitzJames.

contained over 500 volumes, and these not only Latin
Fathers, school men, law, chronicle, and books of
devotion, but authors like Boethius, Virgil, Plato,
Porphyry, Aristotle, Priscian, Persius, Claudian, with
astronomers, geographers, musicians, and even dic-
tionaries. A century later half that number of books
was accounted a magnificent library, and even a hundred
volumes was surprising.

Since Adam's successor built two barns, one at Street
and one at Nettleton in Wilts, we may conclude that
the great barn of Glastonbury was built by Adam de
Sodbury. It is a magnificent one, indeed, in the form
of a cross, with traceried windows and four panels of
the Evangelists. If this is so, we may further conclude
that the two weather-worn statues on the gables are
our Lady of Glastonbury and Father Adam himself.
It is wonderful that the Protestant piety, so reverent
to the barn and the cook-house, should have spared the
holy Gospellers and the statues on this roof, when so
much else was laid low : but corn and pudding are of
universal interest, and awaken a catholic spirit even in
those who are least aware of it. The barn is worth a
visit, if only to see that the Grace of Life which flows
from the Head reaches to the most outward things and
consecrates the very skirts of human life with beauty.

In 1335, another monk, the prior of the House, John
de Brimpton, became Abbot, and ruled for six years.
He was probably of the Glamorgan family, and was not
only an ardent builder of edifices now wholly wiped out,
but was interested in law, glass and jewelry. The
taxation of Edward III was heavy, and the long

struggle with France had begun to tell heavily upon English finances, so that his beautiful hall, kitchen, domestic offices, and elegant steps to the orchard were no small achievement of his prior days, and his great hall, abbot's chapel, long chamber, were well begun, with provisions of wrought timber and glass. He had a strong and orderly rule, although the evil feud with the bishop and other law suits still continued. It is now that we hear of a special Hall at Oxford of four chambers, for the Glastonbury scholars, who were not, like most Benedictine students, lodged in Gloucester College. The provision of a special house (and of a processional cross) does not imply that these students began to be sent to the University then, but does seem to imply that there were, say, a score of them who were now collected into one corporation, until the dissolution put a stop to this excellent work.

Walter de Monington (1341–1374) obtained a peaceful inheritance, and presided over the Abbey for thirty-three eventful and important years. He enlarged the choir by lengthening it to the East, keeping the peculiar character of the church, that strange blend of pointed arch with Norman moulding, but his capitals are distinct. Both Walter and his learned brother Hugh were afterwards buried in the South Transept, and were filled with the enthusiasm for the place, which the sons of so splendid an Alma Mater never failed to show. The man who built these two arches, and vaulted the choir in stone, saw the triumph of Cressy, Neville's Cross, the horrors of the Black Death, and Poitier's battle, when King John was led as a prisoner to Somerton.

He lived through the gradual defeat of the English in France, and saw the beginning both of the great labour troubles and the disturbance of thought which centred around the name of Wicklif. Of these, the most far-reaching was certainly the great pestilence. Of the Abbey livings, nearly one-half lost their priest, and a third lost two priests. The dreadful mortality caused such a dearth of clergy, that the standard of life and learning was deplorably lowered, to meet which, noble efforts were made to found schools and colleges. Church rules were relaxed. Wages and stipends rose, and a long antagonism began between landlords and labourers, bishops and clergy, and even between monks and abbots. So far as we can gather, there were no labour troubles ever at Glastonbury, but Abbot Walter developed that astonishing and significant habit of giving monies to the monks for private possession, which, to men like St. Martin, was so profoundly abhorrent. The 40 senior " priests " (not all monks, for there were many secular clerks in the House) had each 13s. 4d. and ten others half that sum, from the rent of a close called Paradise.[1] The bread and pence of the poor were also increased. The pestilence dealt a great blow to government, learning, and social life at this time, which is, indeed, the turning point in modern history, so that drastic changes were often of compulsion rather than choice. But the fortifications, which the bishop of Bath and Wells had to erect around his palace to protect himself against his exasperated townsmen and rural parishioners, thanks to his active measures in

[1] About £8 and £4 of our money.

reducing trade profits and labourers' wages, were not necessary to the abbots for another hundred years. Not only the social, but the natural fabrics now seemed convulsed. We read of the great gale of Jan. 9, 1362, of the frost which lasted next year from September till April, and of other disasters. Abbot Walter's panelling of the great church was inspired by Gloucester Cathedral, and the connection with Gloucester was

Ruin of Almonry, XV Century near the Abbot's Kitchen.
See page 51.

of old standing, since Edmund the Elder had been brought to be buried in the Abbey, and Pucklechurch, where he was slain, was granted to the place of his burial. That the Church in Somerset should find means for so much work in such a time, is certainly astonishing, but less so if we remember that the corn-growing counties were then far the richest and most populous in England. Norfolk, Lincolnshire, Suffolk, Kent and Somerset, head the list in the church taxes of the Parliament of Westminster, in this order.

The next Abbot, John Chinnock, also had a long and difficult reign (1374–1420), of which small traces remain. Of his greater abbey buildings, not one stone is now standing, and those who would, in fancy, reconstruct his great hall, chapter house, dormitory, and fratry,

must study Bubwith's chantry and the North-West
tower at Wells. With some hesitation, the Abbot's
kitchen may be accredited to him, for a casual notice
shows it to have been standing in his successor's time.
It was erected to maintain the splendid hospitality of
the Abbot to his great guests. The instinctive sympathy
of Protestants spared this noble cook-house, when the
Altars of God were hewn down, and it was still further
honoured by becoming a Quaker's Meeting House in
the XVII Century. The chimneys are gone, but the
fine double lantern remains, as do the four fireplaces,
and the little browning ovens. The effigy of an Abbot
was dug up, and placed there by the piety or wit of 1780.
So far from the Convent thinking highly of this
beautiful building, it is not directly mentioned in the
chronicles. The traces of a screen or division remind
us that the place was enlarged or contracted according to need, for the Abbot's household, large as it was,
did not need more than a part of the kitchen's good
offices. Is there any real need that any kitchen
should be ugly ? or that those Christians who minister to
the hungry, should of necessity do so in gloomy cellars ?

Chinnock has the praise of dull annals, which in the
reigns of Richard II, Henry IV, and Henry V, is no
slight thing.

A local disturbance at Bridgwater was all that troubled
Somerset during Wat Tyler's rebellion. The Abbot
attended the wonderful Parliament, and that which
voted for Richard's resignation ; but neither war nor
lollardry came near his House. The decline in papal
power perhaps caused him to welcome the alliance

which Henry IV made with the church and sealed the friendship for the Red Rose, the cause of legitimist and absolute rule in politics, which was also the cause of great landlords against merchant townsmen. John Chinnock must have met Geoffrey Chaucer, knight of the shire, and forester of North Petherton, a good many times, and it may be but fancy, yet one seems to see in the manly hunting monk of the Canterbury Tales, with his grey hounds, grey fur, and gold pin headed with a love knot, who was ' to ben an abbot able,' who had a shining bald head, and ' anoynt face,' who loved fat swan, and old tales of history, more than a possible portrait of one whom it would be safer to describe as a monk. " He was a lord ful fat, and in good poynt." The two acts for burning heretics, and the Convocation which condemned Sawtre, were attended by this Abbot, whose age, in spite of Agincourt, was one of inward decay, not to be remedied by external compulsion.

Chinnock's successor, Nicholas Frome (1420–45), is a more conspicuous figure. A fragment of his house of mercy or almonry survives, as also the infirmary which he endowed, which is now the almshouse for men in Magdalen Street. But of the chapter-house he finished, of the great chamber and the bishop's chamber, there is nothing. This last is interesting, because it seems to mark an approach to friendlier relations with the See, which we should not gather from Bishop Beckington's harsh and contemptuous letter to the Abbot, when he became old and blind. It is even more significant, that Nicholas found it necessary to surround the abbey

with a great embattled wall. A glance at the portion
now standing to the South will convince the visitor
that this was not a matter of ornament. It made the
Abbey into a fortress, and tells of the disturbed state
of England in the middle of Henry VI's reign, when
heavy taxation for the unlucky French war,[1] lollardry
and faction had produced great distress, and even
danger. It is no wonder that a wall was needed, for
in Jack Cade's rebellion in 1450, William Ascoth, bishop
of Salisbury, was murdered at Edington, only 24 miles
away, his clothes cut to shreds, and his goods distri-
buted among the Commons. It is possible that the wall
had an internal, as well as an external use, for the religious life was very numb at this period. The monks
had ceased to labour and to invent. They increased
their private possessions. The celebrant was given 2d.
for singing High Mass, the same for a Mary Mass, and
4d. for a Requiem. This, in itself, seems to put a world
of difference between the later developments and the
old aim of St. Benedict, expressed in words still em-
bedded in our Litany, " to give to all Thy people increase of grace, to hear meekly Thy word, to receive
it with pure affection, and to bring forth the fruits of
the Spirit." The school, however, still flourished, and
the Oxford students found a protector in Humphrey,
Duke of Gloucester, when they were assaulted and
hindered in their studies.

Nicholas Frome was one of the English envoys to
the great Council of Basle, which began in 1431, and
ended in Florence in 1447. It made a real attempt

[1] Joan was burnt in 1431.

at reform and reconciliation, with concessions to the
Bohemians, such as allowing the Holy Cup to the
laity, which had been disallowed in A.D. 1175. It
almost succeeded in healing the great breach with the
Greeks, and before the English envoys reached Basle
(Aug. 5th, 1434), it had tried to establish the great
principle that General Councils are above Popes, to
which in the 17th Session, Eugenius IV had given
his adhesion. The defeat of this doctrine in later history is the ultimate explanation of the great crash
and confusion of the next century. The English envoys
arrived with a great escort of cavalry, and 150 of the
renowned archers ; but a letter from King Henry VI,
upbraiding the Councillors for their treatment of the
Pope, shows that the influence of our country was on
the side of Absolutism. When the decree was passed,
deposing Eugenius (June 25, 1439), Abbot Nicholas was
not present.

The sack of Constantinople by the Turks on May
29th, 1453, was an event of even more importance.
Pope Nicholas V, who more than any man in Europe
was alive to this disaster, sent confessors to all the
cathedrals and abbies, to offer " the grettyste pardon
that evyr come to Inglonde from the Conqueste unto
thys tyme " to penitents, who confessed their sins, and
paid money for the Crusade, which he tried to kindle.
The enthusiasm of this Pope for the literary treasures
of the East, brought new learning into all the centres
of Western education, and not least to Glastonbury,
where a scholarly life was always possible, and always
encouraged.

Walter More, the next Abbot, lived only a few weeks, and another long reign began with John Selwood (1456-93), who presided through the Wars of the Roses and showed the traditional sympathy of the House by entertaining Queen Margaret and her troops, in that eleven weeks' Lancastrian revolution (in the spring of 1471), which was ended bloodily by the fight at Tewkesbury, and the murder of poor King Henry. This Abbot took Nicholas for his model, and continued the distribution of pocket money at the obits, not only to the secular priests who served some of the altars, but to the monks. The Mass fee at St. Andrew's altar was raised to 4d., to which sum a labourer's day wage had also risen. He also increased the alms for the poor, and the good cheer within. He is credited with building the George or Pilgrim's Inn,[1] and he acquired various properties, among them being Sevenhampton Denys (Seavington), from Edward IV, by an exchange. This, and King Edward's arms on the inn and the Tribunal, seem to prove that the House was not so Lancastrian as to refuse friendship with the King *de facto*. In truth, it has been pointed out that in the unsettled state of the country, vested interests naturally coalesced. One of Abbot John's friends was the cheerful and accommodating Dr. Hugh Sugar, treasurer of Wells, who was

---

[1] John of Glaston says that he bought two tenements by the shambles, and one to the east of the new Inn called the Georges Inn. He also says that he mercifully gave this Inn for the relief of the office of Camerarius, which he found in deplorable ruin. A further note upon the Inn is given later, but it is interesting to remember that Whytyng was Camerarius, before he was Abbot.

either greatly wronged, or a great rogue. He encouraged the malversation of Cathedral funds for the oyster feasts of the *bon vivants* of the Liberty, and accumulated to himself many pleasant offices, held no doubt *sine curâ*. He was a favourite with the powerful. Bishop Beckington, Edmund Duke of Somerset, and Abbot Nicholas all preferred him, the last bestowing the (still plump) living of Lympsham upon him. When Dr. Hugh died in 1489, an obit was kept in his memory at Glastonbury. On his side, he has carved the Abbey arms in his chantry at Wells, so that the mutual friendship is well recorded.

It was in this Abbacy, we may suppose, that the crypt of St. Mary's Chapel was constructed, for the purposes of not unprofitable burial. The floor was raised, the altar moved west, and the well taken into the crypt. This architectural audacity is more in keeping with the husbandry of Selwood than the scholarly activities of his successor. In fact, we have now reached the low-water mark of the great Benedictine House. Riches had increased, but art, handicraft, spiritual and missionary zeal, possibly even learning and book-copying were diminished. Greatness had given way to bigness. The monied monks travelled and wore lay clothes. Archbishop Bourchier's complaints, in 1463, were not directly descriptive of this House, but applied to the evil fashions in vogue in all. He rates the regulars for running abroad in coped caps, and what we should now call fur motor coats. They had monstrous clothes, with stuffed shoulders or bolsters, wore short jackets to the waist, and long beaked shoes scandalously fashionable. Their swords, daggers and pouches were chased with gold. Some even went untonsured, " with nourished hair." Even if we grant that such defects and excesses were found in so magnificent a House, still there was much good to place in the other scale. It was much to superintend great agricultural and commercial works, to see that holidays were not filched from the people, that weights were just, beer of sound quality without substitutes, that folk were judged, policed, defended, cherished, nursed, employed, relieved, decently housed, provided with roads, bridges, sea walls, lights (or benefit and insurance societies without absconding secretaries), infirmaries, hospitality and alms. Besides these, there were the effective educational ladders, and not least, the whole Means of Grace, joyfully and splendidly set forth for all. The worst days of the Abbey never withheld from the poor the best things of their time and of all time, so scornfully and completely as the " more enlightened ages " have done. The old labourers still speak of the monks as " a wonderful good class of people served terrible bad," and their tradition is sound. It was not they, but the large farmer, who told Hannah More that " religion never did good to agriculture, since the monks down at Glastonbury brought it in," which saying meant that the interest of the poor was never better served, before or since. Selwood presided through the decadent days of Edward IV, saw the tragedy of Edward V and his brother (the babes in the wood, or Princes in the Tower), and lived through the short clever, pathetic reign of Richard. In spite of wars, taxes, and benevolences, forbidden but kept, he managed to increase the income by £62 per annum, close on £1,000 of our money. The support Henry Tudor obtained from legitimist Houses is not likely to have been warm ; but Lambert Simnel got no overt help. Yet the fact that Archbishop Morton obtained a Bull for visiting all exempt and privileged monasteries, shows and engendered great friction between these and the Crown. The sweating sickness, brought in by Henry's mercenaries, was active in the warm misty West. It was not quite so fatal in Somerset as elsewhere, but a disease that closed the University of Oxford for a time, was a great hindrance to education. Selwood's reign thus closed in gloom. The honour of the House was bound up with its learning, and the Prior, Thomas Wason, being learned, the monks made an abortive attempt to elect him. This election was happily quashed by Richard Fox, that splendid promoter of learning. The founder of Taunton Grammar School and of Corpus Christi College at Oxford, was no enemy to education or the revival of letters, so that his action is justified in the event. In 1493, the greatest abbot since St. Dunstan was chosen in Wason's place. This was Richard Beere (1493–1524), who, like many of the abbots, came of gentle Somerset blood. The de Beers came from Cannington. Richard was a Glastonbury and Oxford scholar, who, after he was abbot, applied for his degree as Doctor of Divinity, perhaps as part of a University contention that monks should be allowed so to graduate, and also because the doctors of a House were much accounted of. Scholar, artist, builder,

sportsman, patron of the Muses and Graces, father to
his people's souls, minds and conditions, this great
man left a mark upon the holy place, which even the
ruin of after years has not wholly obliterated. He
combined a love of the old, with an enthusiasm for the
new learning. He was the friend, helper and, to some
extent, the corrector of Erasmus. Yet he was also an
admirer of the devotion of Loretto, which he had
visited when he went on an embassy to greet Pius
III (1503).[1] On his return he built the Chapel of Our
Lady of Loretto, near to that of St. Thomas, in the North-
East of the nave. He helped St. John's Church to
obtain a number of the new printed books, which were
chained to desks, and open for all to read. He rebuilt
the Chapel of St. Benignus, now a Parish Church. He
set up an almshouse for women, with a chapel still
standing, and the Leper Hospital at Taunton now an
almshouse. He began the glorious Chapel of St. Edgar,
finished by his successor, which Mr. Bligh Bond has
shown to have been 49 feet long (with a probable ex-
tension of 24 ft 9 in.), and built it in the style of Henry
VII's Chapel at Westminster, "the premier building
of England." This was a capitular chapel, at the head
of the great Church,[2] for to the student abbot, King
Edgar had held up the head of Christ in his Church.
There is something much akin between these two rapid,
energetic determined men, parted as they are by five

[1] The Chiesa della Casa Santa was built for Paul II in 1465,
but the dome over the holy Cottage was erected by Giuliano da
Sangallo in 1500.

[2] The usual position of the Lady Chapel, for Our Lady upheld
Christ's head.

centuries. If we interpret Erasmus' letter rightly in his humorous address of *amplitudo tua*, he tells us that Beere, like Edgar, was of very short stature, and addicted to hunting, as the metaphors in the same letter suggest. Soon after Beere's consecration, the Cornish rebels, under Lawyer Flamoke and Farrier Joseph, passed through from Taunton to Wells, in angry revolt at the exactions of the King. Apparently the gates of the Abbey were closed, and they did not stop to climb the great wall, but hurried on to their doom at Blackheath. But Perkin Warbeck's revolt was a more tempting moment for the West to get rid of a plain and covetous usurper, and Glastonbury was mulct in a fine of £428 (heading the county list), when the rebellion failed. Henry did not bear malice long, for he came in person to settle the country (1497), and lodged in " the King's lodgings." He so liked the scholar abbot that he employed him on his service. The lodgings are gone, and so are the rooms for the secular priests, or Clerks of Our Lady, and, of course, the rich antipendium of silver gilt, which was given to emblazon the high altar. But the Tribunal in High Street remains to tell of the goodness of this man's work. In default of precise evidence, we may suppose it to have been built, after the return of the sweating sickness in 1506, when the danger of bringing prisoners and a mixed multitude of witnesses into the precincts would be apparent. Here offenders were judged in that almost royal court, which ruled the twelve hides ; and, if necessary, rogues were confined in the dungeons beneath it. That the Abbot had, at one time, even the power of life and

G

death, is proved *inter alia* by the suit of Elyas *versus*
Matthew de Clevedon, for 40 acres of land in Hemme-
grave, in 1243. The appellant's father had been hanged
as a thief, by Abbot Michael, for stealing three bacons ;
but wrongfully he claimed, and " out of hate and
spite." The Tribunal dungeons are now covered with
a floor, and, being not visible, can excite the easy
disbelief of the captious.[1] Abbot Richard vaulted in
stone " the eastern part of the church," and strengthened
the central piers by the beautiful St. Andrew's cross
supports across the transept and West arches, which
were weakened, no doubt by the bells and the spire.[2]
These arches suggested, of course, by those at Wells,
have been reconstructed by Mr. Bond in his sketch of
the abbey at its prime ; and tell of a combination of
art and science which, in our own time, is often still
to seek. The same builder's idea of a central fan roof
is happily still familiar to us in other buildings. Small
portions of Beere's decoration—his panelled soffit—
may still be seen in the inward span of the giant arch,
and nothing that he touched he failed to adorn. In our
day, Aristotle's virtue of magnificent expenditure is
looked upon as suspect and splendour held to contra-
dict saintliness. In Beere's time, luxury did not mean
the resources of intelligence and civilization, and he
would have been astonished to have the epithet luxurious,
because he rode through life like a prince, and built
wherever he lodged, as at Sharpham, ceiled houses full

[1] See additional note on Tribunal, page 92.

[2] Spire and not tower, because of the representation in the
Abbey seal.

of pleasantness. But he never ground the faces of the poor, as may be seen from the fact that he had twenty families of serfs at Doulting—thriving farmers in reality, who did not wish to buy themselves free, until there was a threat of lay proprietorship, when they all did so with alacrity.[1] This Abbot's splendour is shown by the fact that he had, besides his Glastonbury and London lodging, ten manour houses for his reception and entertainment. He had hounds, hawks, and horses in abundance. Yet he ruled with great diligence, and travelled over every part of his great domain, making a careful terrier of what he had in trust. All the best men of his day were reformers, and he must be ranked with Fisher, Colet, More, Erasmus, and the younger better Wolsey, to whom he was well known and dear. As he was also a great Greek scholar and critic, we may be sure that his school was refreshed by these wider studies, and gained in renown accordingly. He was alive, though not present, at the Field of the Cloth of Gold ; but he took an active part in the reception of Charles V, on his memorable visit to England in 1522, rode in the Cardinal's train, and met the Emperor at Dover, and escorted him to Richmond. The very bills of fare are with us for the 208 gentlemen of the train.[2] With dainties, and a speech by Sir Thomas More, an

[1] There were 271 bondmen at the dissolution.

[2] For dinner—(i) Pottage, Boyled Capon, Gr sh (?), Young Vele, Grene Gese, Kyde, Custards, Fruttour ; (ii) Jussell, Chykyns, Peions, Rabettes, Tarte. For supper—(i) Potage, Chykyns Boyled, Jegges of Motton, Capons, Kyde, Dowcettes ; (ii) Jely, Ipocras, Peions, Chykyns, Rabettes, Tartes. Copious Rhemish and Gascon wines washed down this fare.

entente cordiale was established with the Emperor, to
the indignation of France. But before the Battle of
Pavia, Abbot Richard had laid down his mortal body,
directing it to be buried near the Chapel of the Holy
Sepulchre, which he had erected in the great church,
Crusader that he was. For all his grandeur, he chose
to lie *sub plano marmore*, under one smooth slab,
unadorned. He could not have been over fifty years
of age when he died, and was happy not to have lived
another fifteen, as he might easily have done. The
Lane to the South of the Abbey is called after this
active Abbot, who left peace behind him, and what
then seemed a settled and established foundation.
The success of this Abbacy was great, but it was a
personal success. It was the triumph of a gallant,
learned, efficient, vigorous man, rather than of the
methods and principles which he advocated, for the
success stopped short immediately the master died.

The monks in their wish to preserve the activity,
renown, and (autumnal) popularity of their House, re-
quested the Lord Cardinal Wolsey to choose an Abbot
for them. He had been a friend to the late Abbot,
and he had known Glastonbury for many years, for he
was rector of Lymington, Nr. Ilchester (1500–1509),
and after that bishop of the revenues of Bath and Wells
(1518–23). The later faults of Wolsey have blinded
people to his earlier virtues. He was filled with high
ideas, a favourer of learning, a patron of artists, and
of holy living. His friends were the best men of the
day. He was a sincere reformer, and a preacher of reform in schools and in the Church, and was anxious to

correct the faults in the latter, and especially " of the
inferior clergy by all the means he could think of,
except the giving of them a good example." But court
manners, court suppleness, and a great devotion to
himself and to his aspirations, were now the qualities
he required most, in those whom he patronized. He
therefore bid the monks to elect their old chamberlain,
whose courtesies to guests he must have known long
since. This was Richard Whytyng, a Cambridge Doctor,
who, since he took his M.A. in 1483, when Wolsey was
eight, must have been well over 60 years of age. He
seems to have been a good natured, polished, learned
chamberlain, with no determination of character, no
passionate devotion to pure ideas, but gentle, amiable,
and courteous. Perhaps, the greatest passion of his
life was a love of the gallant, great Benedictine House,
in which he had served and ruled. Possibly the best
that can be said of him is that, though he was Wolsey's
friend, Sir Thomas More held a corrody in the Abbey,
and could get battels there at need. If the way had
ever opened for that winsome scholar to adopt the
religious life to which he was much inclined, certainly
he would have ended his days here. Under Whytyng,
who had been himself a Master of the School, Beere's
educational work was continued. It was claimed that
300 nobles and gentry had passed through his hands,
beside many others of meaner origin, on their way to
the Universities and the priesthood.[1] A useful and

---

[1] Considering the man's age, this need not astonish us. It
required no large school to educate 600 pupils, in a possible 40
years or more. A school of modest numbers—say 45—would

orderly life, with wide sympathies and great concessive powers, was a small equipment for an abbot in these stormy and evil times. Whytyng was in Beere's shoes, but not in his junior's mantle. He finished St. Edgar's Chapel, as Beere would have had it finished : but St. Edgar was the champion of English monasticism, and the chapel was an assertion of the value of this life, in days when it was freely challenged. The state and pomp of Beere was kept up. The retinue of a hundred retainers, the hawks and dogs were continued, but the old Abbot was a stay at home man, and unless called to Convocations and Parliaments, he did not travel. This means that the great domain was the less effectively governed, the more criticism and discontent grew. There is evidence of constant friction. The game was heavily poached. The 800 head of deer at Sharpham were shot down by no mean persons. The mews were invaded, and the fat capons and cygnets purloined ; and the Abbot was full of apologies for taking action against the thieves. At the last, the tenants were eager to join in the assault upon the muddling old ruler, and the gentry about condemned him without a murmur. Perhaps, being like Wolsey, of no family and having married his niece Alice to a noble feudatory of the Abbey, Strode of West Cranmere, he had ruffled their prejudices for he fell, almost it would seem without a friend, but with the many bitter enemies which inefficiency and weakness always breed. After five years of anxious rule, during which he must have pined for the

suffice, if the pupils stayed for a three years' course. Talk about the University of the West is mere clap-trap.

modest income of the George, and his lighter office of chamberlain, Whytyng found that the evil question of the divorce had alienated the King from his friend Wolsey. The overtaxed people, under More, thereupon opposed and upset the policy of extravagance and autocracy, which, ephemeral as it was bound to be, in Wolsey's hands, kept the peace between King and Pope. In 1529, the Abbot transferred his homage to the rising Chancellor, for which he got little love from Wolsey's faithful unscrupulous friend, Thomas Cromwell. In 1531, the Universities had given their replies. The marriage with Katharine was declared—in England— to be unlawful. To the sorrow of the clergy, a divorce was pronounced. The lawyers then turned upon the clergy, and proved them all guilty of *Præmunire*, by implication with Wolsey. To escape from confiscations, the clergy including the Abbot, accepted, in silence, the King's title as " Protector and Supreme Head of the Church and Clergy of England," and bought themselves off with a heavy fine. To help them pay this, the Parliament of 1532, with professions of humble loyalty to the Church, restrained annates, or handing to the Pope one year's profit of livings. Convocation (and Whytyng) submitted more fully to the King ; promised to enact no new canon without his leave, and to revise the old ones. In June, 1533, Queen Anne was crowned, with unheard-of rejoicings, pomps and pageants, bishops, nobles abbots, and all the great men of England joining, without the least jar, in denying thus the Papal dispensing power and curtailing his authority. The Pope immediately declared

the marriage of Katharine valid. The counter move
was the restraint of appeals to Rome, with the assertion
that England, spiritual and temporal, was able to
determine her own cases. In 1534, these appeals were
overtly forbidden, Abbot's Courts were made subject
to Chancery,[1] bishops were to be chosen by royal
missive, papal dispensations and the payment of
Peter's pence were forbidden. Anne's marriage and
Elizabeth's legitimacy were accepted, and the King
was declared " the only supreme head in earth of the
Church of England " ; and, moreover, it was further
decided that he had power to visit ecclesiastically.
The lawyers quieted the uneasy country by saying
that no new precedents were created, that Henry
claimed no more than had been granted long ago ;
but the remorseless Cromwell knew that " the fallacy of
division " was not enough to hinder revolt. An oath of
fealty to the royal pair was exacted. A reign of terror,
with spies, blackmail, and perjury set in. It was treason
to call the King heretic, schismatic tyrant or usurper :
and the worst of miseries was, as Tacitus said of the
Domitian terror, even men's sighs were noted against
them. Still the Abbot acquiesced and voted aye. In
July, More, Fisher and the Charter House monks refused
the oath, and went gallantly to death. Yet in September, Whytyng and all his monastery without ex-
ception, swore fealty to Henry and Anne his wife,
agreed that the King was head of the English Church,
that " the Bishop of Rome, who in his bulls usurps the

---

[1] Whytyng only pointed out that a deadlock ensued, but did
not protest.

name of Pope, and the dominion of chief bishop has
no more jurisdiction given him by God in this realm of
England, than has any other foreign bishop." They
also renounced all Canon Law, that conflicted with
Civil Law and bound themselves always to speak of
the Pope as Bishop of Rome. More than half of the
monks signed second names, taken from the saints
connected, by breeding or relics, with Glastonbury.
None refused this terrific oath.

Meantime, the visitation of monasteries was proceed-
ing apace with the utmost rigour. Monks who had
been professed under 25, were turned out of doors,
goods were catalogued, and every evil tale of every
discontented slanderer eagerly noted, by a crew of
scoundrels. The black book was flourished in Parliament, and (1536) the smaller monasteries were dissolved,
just as " Anne our Queen " was found to be no queen
and no wife, but only a hysterical traitress, to be herself
betrayed and butchered. This same year, the ancient
immunities of abbies were abolished, without protest,
while Convocation, under the King and Cromwell's
direction, passed the Articles of Religion, in which the
Romish (but not the Catholic) doctrine of purgatory was
attacked, and the trade of papal pardoners entirely
abolished. This, too, was signed *Richardus ab. Glas-
coniæ*. The Lincoln and Northern rebellions were the
immediate reply of the people to these assaults, and to
this system. The latter, or Pilgrimage of Grace, has
been explained by the great severity of the new landlords, and the failure of the poor-relief. It was too
immediate for such causes. It was a genuine movement

for the ending of the Domitian terror, for the super-
seded Papal authority, and for the ill-used despised
monks and monasticism. For a long time the issues
were doubtful, and it is impossible not to feel that the
hearts of all the great religious Houses must have been
with Aske, and their funds secretly at his service. The
poor old Abbot Whytyng, at this time, was granting
manours, concessions, advowsons, and probably copious
commissions to the wolfish and covetous plunderers,
who ringed him round. The fine report of Glastonbury, with its good discipline and strait keeping, was
doubtless bought dear, and is as valuable as the grovel-
ling apology for drawing it up, which the same creature
wrote later. It has the value of Dr. Layton's other
verdicts, and they all have the value of that Cambridge
cynic's life, which was shameful, even in a most dis-
reputable age. 318 Religious houses were forcibly and
indecently suppressed. On the 243 which remained,
the pressure to surrender was enormous. Discipline
was dissolved, faith perplexed, revenue shrunken,
sympathy alienated, mockery and insult encouraged.
No wonder that promises and pensions on the one
hand, and ugly threats on the other, prevailed on many
men in such straits. In 1539 came the Act for the
dissolution of the greater Monasteries, either by
voluntary surrender, or by attainder of treason.
The same Parliament also passed the celebrated Six
Articles. This was not attended by Whytyng, who
wrote to be excused, saying that he was greatly
diseased, and could only move in great pain, with a
staff, but to please the King, would be if necessary,

carried up to Westminster in a horse-litter. As he showed no signs of surrendering the holy earth to certain desecration and defilement, the weak old man was cynically marked for death,[1] although he had been so ceaselessly complying with the royal will. Many great people, such as Sir John FitzJames, Dame Katharine Dawbynaye and Leland, bear witness to the Abbot's white life and personal piety, and though he was not popular among the general, yet one must remember that the wrongs caused by inefficiency are great, and smart as much as do those of malice. The end must have astonished the tenants, who " put up bills against him for wrongs he had done them " : it came with surprising suddenness. But before we look at the final scenes, there are two or three glimpses into the Abbey we have, belonging to these last years. An organist, Renynger by name, was appointed to sing and play the organ, and other instruments at Christmas, to teach six children " pricke song and descaunte," and two of them to play the organ. The monastery found " clavyng-cordes " for the scholars, and gave the organist £10 a year, a gown or 13s. 4d., two loads of wood, and a house rent free, or another 13s. 4d.—which, as things went, was a handsome honorarium.[2] Sir Thomas More's corrody was given to Richard Snell, a yeoman of the king's guard, some relative of Sir John Snell's, perhaps ; but there were men of this name in Foxe's Martirs, and from Scotland to the South Coast. In 1536, a friar called John Brynstan, created some

---

[1] In the fashion of *Il Principe*.

[2] Did Renynger compose any Masses or Antiphons ?

stir by preaching in the Abbey Church, and boasting
that he would convert the new fangles and new men,
or die in the quarrel : but he expounded the king's
title of head, to his great honour, and the utter for-doing
of the bishop of Rome." [1]

Perhaps Abbot Whytyng (like his brothers of Reading
and Colchester) hoped for something from the Six
Articles passed in June. Anyhow, he made no signs of
surrender. In September, the Commissioners swept
down again upon Glastonbury, and found the Abbot
at Sharpham Park. Everything was ransacked. His
books and papers were seized. A good deal of hidden
treasure was unearthed, and some material, " we think
to be very high and rank treasons "—the details of
which are lost. The two treasurers, Prior John Thorne
and Roger James (Brothers John Arthur and Roger
Wylfryd) and two secular clerks, were also seized. The
poor old man was hurried off to the Tower, tried there,
and sent down to Wells " to be tried and executed,"
that is, re-tried. There is not a tittle of sound evidence, [2]
that the Supremacy question was raised at either trial.
It was " the very high and rank treasons " found
in the papers, which convinced these two sets of jurors.
The hiding of monies was not legally treason. It could
be made into felony, by an unwholesome quibble :
but " as worsshipfull a jurye as was charged there

[1] Dom Gasquet cites this, with the latter part excised, to
show how Whytyng allowed " a doctrine by no means in accord
with the royal theories." It shows the exact opposite.

[2] Except the first desires of Sander and others of his views ;
and a too hasty acceptation of these by Godwin, Collier, and
others.

theis many yeres," would not have done to death an
old man, for stowing away his cups and cash. Corre-
spondence with rebels in the Pilgrimage of Grace, or
with some others in Somerset, who made an abortive
rising in March, would give colour to the verdict, without postulating a sudden martyr-spirit in one who had
never shown a spark of it for seventy years. There is
a legend that, misled by the hypocrisy of his gaolers,
the bewildered old man at Wells thought the bitterness
of death was past, and was about to sit upon the Board,
which last tried him. Anyhow, he was condemned on
Nov. 14th, taken to Glastonbury, where he lay, that
night, as we may suppose, in the Tribunal dungeon,
with the two monks. Next day, they were all drawn
on hurdles to the Tor, hanged, disembowelled, beheaded,
and quartered. The poor old Abbot's white head was
set over the gate, and his quarters, boiled in pitch, were
displayed at Wells, Bath, Ilchester and Bridgwater.

THE DESTRUCTION AND AFTER

WHILST poor Richard Whytyng was taking his
death patiently upon the Tor, the destruction
of the great Church and House had already begun.
The monks and servants were dismissed, the holy relics
sent in bags to the King. The lead was stripped off
the roof, and used for Jersey Castle. "Every person
had everything good cheap, except the poor monks."

The demolition of Roche Abbey (described by an eye-witness of the fate), may tell us of them all. Locks, shackles, and bolts were wrenched away, and the very doors were carried off. " Some took the Service Books that lied in the Church, and laid them upon their waine coppes to peice the same : some took windows of the Haylath, and hid them in their hay ; and likewise they did of many other things ; for some pulled forth iron hooks out of the walles that bought none, when the yeomen and gentlemen of the country had bought the timber of the church. For the church was the first thing that was put to the spoil ; and then the Abbot's lodging, dorter and Frater, with the cloister and all the buildings thereabouts ; for nothing was spared, but the ox-houses and swine-coates, and such other houses of office, that stood without the walls ; which had more favour showed them than the very church itself : which was done by the advice of Cromwell, as Fox reporteth in his Book of Acts and Monuments."[1] It would have pitied any heart to see what tearing up of the lead there was, and plucking up of the boards, and throwing down of sparres ; and when the lead was torn off and cast down into the church, and the tombs in the church all broken (for in most Abbeys were divers noble men and women, yea, and in some Abbeys Kings, whose tombs were regarded no more than the tombs of all other inferior persons : for to what end should they stand, when the church over them was not spared for their cause), and all things of price either spoiled, carped away, or defaced to the uttermost." The indignant

[1] Cf. Barn and Kitchen.

writer, who may be read in Ellis, 3rd Series, III 31, describes the burning of carved oak Misereres, tells of pewter vessels filched and hidden, bells broken and education at a stand. " Thus you may see that as well they that thought well of the Religion then used, as they which thought otherwise, could agree well enough and too well to spoil them. Such a devil is covetousness and mammon ! " The cattle, furniture, locks, doors, glass windows, iron and timber, were sold at nominal prices. The carved wood hacked to pieces— one bit can be seen in a cottage window in Northlode Street. The stones were sold in cheap cartloads for all purposes. Worst of all, the books and manuscripts of the matchless library were sold by weight to binders and grocers ; torn up and used for parcels, fires, and every dishonest purpose. The poor stole handfuls, the rich filched farms and manours. " Little Jack Horner," one of Whytyng's judges, secured Mells, a legend says by concealing the deeds in a pie dish, which he covered with bread for the needy, and so conveyed them away.

Perhaps, one of the saddest things of all this desecration is the little stir which it made. Men believed that there would be no more taxes, if once the Monasteries were made over to the King. Alas ! they were more quickly converted to the truth in that, than in most things. The Somerset poor had been cowed already by Lord Willoughby's action in the West. The wealthy got plums and self-applause. Many of the richer trading classes were already strong Protestants, and the death of the three abbots was met by a shout of glee, from the adopters of religions made in Germany. Butler writes

to Bullinger that " the Abbots are rotting on gibbets,
a worthy recompense for their imposture." Edward
VI's reign, with its spoliation of the Guilds and Lights,
that pitiless grab at the savings of the poor, must have
deepened men's regrets for the mercy which built the
fair old House. The communicants then were 700 in
number ; they are now 429. [1]

The filchings and cheap bargains came dear in the end
for the town was nothing without the Abbey. Consequently the Duke of Somerset (Arviragus II, in his own
eyes) settled a company of Walloon worsted weavers
in the ruins, and with greater rural wisdom than some
have shown since, gave five acres and two cows to each
of these 38 families. These people cut down the walnut,
which came out on St. John's Day. The Somerset
people, who do not like strange faces and tongues,
hated and cheated them. Even their agents did the
same. The foreigners were unable to make for themselves any permanent trade, and were chased off under
Queen Mary to Frankfurt. The weaving was taken up
by local people, and survived for a long time, but only
in a small way.

It is sometimes asserted that some of the monks
went over to San Malo, and continued the House there ;
France doing for England then, what England now does
for her. But the Benedictine House there has neither
books, relics, nor tradition of this source, and was in
fact founded in 1606, by two Englishmen, Gifford and
Barnes long after Glastonbury lay desolate.

It is astonishing that almost none of the relics, jewels,

[1] St. John, 310; St. Benignus, 119 ; Easter, A.D. 1908.

Ancient Stone Altar in St. Patrick's Chapel of the
Women's Almshouses.

See page 89.

The Tribunal.
See pages 59 *and* 92.

or portable art works can now be traced. St. David's great sapphire passed to the Crown. It may have been in the pawned regalia which Queen Henrietta Maria left in France. It may have been the great sapphire which Cardinal York gave to George III, which George IV allowed Lady Conyngham to wear in her hair : but the keeper of the Crown jewels has no information to give. Granted that these guesses be true, has it served any better purposes than when it glowed in the Altar of the Mother of God ?

The thorn from the Saviour's Crown is in St. Mary's Abbey at Stanbrook, near Worcester, and there is one relic in the Museum, of St. Paulinus.

The manuscripts and books are gone so completely that the British Museum can only claim a (Cottonian) List of relics, (Additional) H. Bracton De juribus, and a perquisite book of Walter de Monington. The Bodleian has some Irish Canons of IX Century, and Dunstan's Augustine on the Revelation, and his Canons and the (Auct. F. N. 32) book, with the Saint's picture of himself worshipping, engraved in Hick's Thesaurus, a few cartularies, and possibly some printed books.

The other results of the Dissolution were unhappy. Instead of nearly £3 a week in alms (£30 of our money), with good schooling and much help for scholars, we hear a positive wail go up, " Nowe charitie is waxed cold, none helpeth the scholer nor yet the pore." Dr. Layton sneeringly said that Glastonbury had but three bachelours of Divinity, and those slenderly learned. Latimer gives a far worse story of the new men. " If the ploughemen of the countrey were as negligente in

H

theyr office as prelates be, we shoulde not longe lyue for lacke of sustinaunce."

In Queen Mary's reign, four pathetic monks, then lodged in Westminster, petitioned for the House and site and no more, with leave to live in their habits there among the people, " so affected to our Religion," who would help them " prevent the ruin of much, and repair no little part of the whole." Cardinal Pole even thought of putting Jesuits there : but the Queen's death upset all plans. It thus seems evident the buildings were still in some completeness of shell, up to the reign of Elizabeth. But the water ways were not kept in repair and the sea banks not looked to : so that the people might well sigh for the old order, and resent the new. A Puritan finding the Holy Thorn on Wirrial hill, a stumbling block to his disbelief, cut down one limb ; but to the glee of all malicious persons, maimed himself in the act. His foolish attempt was completed by one of the Roundhead ruffians of a later time ; but not before buds from the thorn had been set in many white-thorns by many hands, of which one survives still in the Abbey grounds. In 1606, the neglected sea banks broke, and the water washed up to St. Benignus Church. During the Civil War, there were several occupations and marches through, but no action at Glastonbury. The place was ranked by the Presbyterians as belonging to the Classis of Wells and Bruton. It had not enthusiasm enough to support a minister, but furnished two elders, Richard Dale and Jeffery Austen, to their organisation. In 1649, the two churches were, for 9 months, in the hands of one John Luffe, who afterwards was called (by the election of arms) to dispossess the Rector of Aylesbury, Master Barton,[1] and being himself set free from his intruded ministry, became thereby a nonconformist martyr at the Restoration. In 1685, Monmouth's troops encamped in the Abbey ruins, *en route* for Bristol. But the greatest event of the XVII Century for Glastonbury was the birth of Thomas Hearne (1678–1735), who was under-keeper of the Bodleian, and a non-juror. This noble man, to the derision of his contemporaries, and the contempt of Pope,[2] rediscovered Glastonbury, and published practically the whole of its surviving chroniclers, so that all other authors since are overwhelmingly in his debt. He edited faithfully and printed pleasantly (*a*) William of Malmesbury (1143) on the Antiquity of the Church, with Adam de Domerham (1291) on Glastonbury doings ;[3] and (*b*) John of Glastonbury's book, with the same title (1400), with William Wyck's sequel up to 1497, with extracts from Beere's terrier, a Use of lights, charters, and lists of goods, papers, books, and relics ;[4] (*c*) A History and Antiquities of Glastonbury,[5] which contains the Roman Catholic Charles Eyston's " Little Monument to the once famous Abbey and Borough, 1716." In days when there were neither Rolls Series, Camden Society, nor State Papers possible for consultation, these and various other shreds and patches

[1] Perhaps Tom Barton, Rupert's Chaplain.

[2] To future ages may thy dulness last,
As thou preserv'st the dulness of the past.
Dun. III, 188.

[3] Oxford, 1727.   [4] Oxford, 1726.   [5] Oxon, 1722.

were works for which lovers of Glastonbury cannot be
too grateful to this most enlightened scholar. In
1724, the Abbey was in the hands of a Presbyterian,
and " every week a pillar, a buttress, a window jamb,
or angle is sold to the best bidder," says William
Stukeley. " Whilst I was there, they were excoriat-
ing St. Joseph's Chapel for that purpose, and the
squared stones were laid up for that purpose in the
Abbot's kitchen. The rest goes to paving yards
and stalls for cattle or the high way." Thus Hearne's
pleadings were none too soon, but rather too late.
Yet they aroused a certain interest, and perhaps
even told the prædatory Presbyterian that he was
turning away money by his hewings and desecration. Folk came to see what was left, and some have
recorded their impressions. Among them, more
lively than the rest, was Miss Fanny Burney (Ap.,
1790). She was bewitched with the antique beauty.
She imagined the tall spire arch to be the main front
of the Abbey, thus showing that even the outline
of the church was now obliterated. " If this monastery was built by the famous old, cruel hypocrite
Dunstan, I shall grieve so much taste was bestowed on
such a wretch." Thus they learned history in Fanny's
century !

Two other events of this century may be noticed.
The birth of Henry Fielding, the Novelist, April 22, 1707,
was in the Harlequin's Chamber, at Sharpham. Dr.
Johnson said he was a blockhead : " What I mean by
his being a blockhead, is that he was a barren rascal."
Yet he has still many admirers, even more than he has

readers. The second incident is the dream of Mat Chancellor, 1750, who learnt that by fasting, prayer, and Chalice water, he might be healed of the asthma. He did as he dreamt, and wheezed no more. Others, some with and some without prayer and fasting, others with faith in the water alone, flocked to the place. To the chagrin of physicians some were cured ; to the chagrin of superstition, more were not cured ; to the chagrin of landladies, licensed victuallers, rate-payers and pump-room persons, the fashion changed. The analytical chemists can discern no charm whereby to attract the diseased public ; and Canon Scott Holmes sees in these waters " little else than waters." In 1826, Richard Warner, the Rector of Great Chalfield, published in Bath his " History of Glastonbury," a valuable untidy book, written in a scornful style, which many of his obliged successors have faithfully reproduced. But as more material is now open to the ordinary student, the struggles, labours, and hopes and prayers of so many generations of Englishmen are less lightly thought about, but the English Jerusalem still waits for its great historian.

In 1908, the Bishop of Bath and Wells (Dr. Kennion), by one of the humours of history, acquired the Abbey site for the Church, and though a score of Abbots would shudder at the thought that their traditional opponent should have bought the sacred acres, we may yet hope that St. Mary's Church will be roofed in, and the Eternal Sacrifice be once more pleaded in this holy spot.

Mr. Bligh Bond, who is in charge of the excavations on behalf of the Somerset Archæological Society, has

already made many important discoveries.[1] He has
determined the architectural form of the Great Church
of SS. Peter and Paul, and of St. Edgar's Chapel. He
has found a skeleton buried in a dropstone, near the
West of the South wall, with another skull between its
feet, which tells of a burial in Roman times, which may
be of one of the first disciples. The remains of a mud and
wattle hut under St. Edgar's Chapel also, may be one
of the cænobite dwellings of the old Laura : and many
fragments of glass and stone will serve to tell strange
stories to such as can read them. He has found the
traces of two Western towers to the great church. It
is now evident that the Church was, after old St. Paul's,
the longest in England, being nearly 600 feet from East
to West. The Abbey was also richer than any other,
being valued at over £3,500, in the Valor Ecclesiasticus,
over a thousand pounds a year more than any other.
But we must multiply money incomes by at least ten,
to get any idea of the wealth of the period compared
to our own.

WIRRIAL AND BECKARY

A S the visitor leaves the railway station he sees
before him Wirrial Hill, already mentioned as
the cattle pasture of the ancient fortress, where St.
Joseph and his companions first rested. On this hill
there is a flat stone to mark the spot, where the Holy

[1] Vol. LIV, Som. Archæological Proceedings.

Thorn once grew. Here was of old a dwelling-place for holy women, with a Chapel of St. Peter and a guest chamber. King Arthur took much delight in this place, and often lodged in it. A little to the West is the low island of Beckary, where was a Chapel of St. Mary Magdalen. Beckary is called Parva Hibernia, little Ireland, because here St. Bridget, after whom so many Irish Biddies are named, passed some years of her life. The foundation of two successive chapels are still in the soil. When St. Bridget returned to Ireland, her wallet, chaplet, bell and weaving tools were treasured in her memory at Glastonbury, and the chapel was re-built and dedicated to her. One memorable day, a cen-tury after St. Bridget, when King Arthur was resting on Wirrial, he heard a voice which told him to rise at daybreak and go to this chapel. Sir Gawaine dissuaded him, but again the voice gave him a second command. At day-break the king sent his chamberlain to the place. The man saw there a corpse, enshrined with four lights around it, and an altar lit by two golden candlesticks. In a fit of covetousness he seized one of these last and hid it in his cloak : but suddenly one appeared to him in wrath, upbraided him, and struck him with a knife in the groin. He had just time to show both candlestick and knife to the king when he died. Arthur approached the place in fear, and saw it was guarded by two hands, holding swords. He kneeled down and cried for mercy and pardon for his sins, and then saw the swords withdrawn. He entered the holy place, and found a white-haired priest, in the armour of God, who saluted him, and began the Mass. Then there stood by that altar as acolyte, the glorious Mother of God, with her Babe in her arms. At the offertory she gave the Divine Word instead of bread, and the priest presented, elevated, sacrificed, and communicated Him, and yet immediately He was whole and unhurt in His Mother's arms. At the end of the service the Mother of God gave the King a cross of crystal, which was kept for centuries in the Abbey. In memory of this vision, the king took for his arms, in his battles with the heathen, on a green field, a silver cross, with the Mother of God and her Son in the first quarter. These were in after days the arms of the Abbey.

ST. BENIGNUS CHURCH AND ST. MARY MAGDALEN'S CHAPEL

Ornamental Boss in St. Benignus Church.

ST. BENIGNUS (fl. A.D 460) was an early disciple of St. Patrick, who, as a tiny babe, kissed the dear Apostle's foot and cried to be with him. In delight at such ardent love St. Patrick named him Benignus, the kind one, instead of Beon. He succeeded his master, and worked in Ireland, until worn with years he followed his teacher's example and came to die at Avalon. He built a hermit's cell at

Ferramere, and died there. In the reign of William Rufus, Abbot Turstin sought out his bones and brought them with great honour, by water to the Abbey. They were wrapped in fine linen, placed in a shrine and rowed up the water-ways in a wonderful light, by a monk and a layman. A great procession, such as Normans loved, bearing banners, crosses, censers and torches, met the boat at the lode, or landing stage. Half-way between this and the Abbey, the procession halted, a sermon was preached, the relics were shown and such Grace and wonders followed the blessing of the people, that a chapel was built on the very spot. It was rebuilt by the active piety of Abbot Beere, whose mitre and initials are on the North Porch : but it has been much disfigured by the bad taste of the Victorian period. The visitor may notice the badge of the Five Wounds on one of the corbels. St. Benignus' was made a parish church in 1846, and has about 1,300 parishioners, but only 119 communicants. The East window in the porch is a rarity, and may have served to light folk to Mass on winter mornings. The niches in the tower once contained statues of St. Benignus, and, perhaps, of St. Benedict, hence the church and street for a time were called after the latter. The poor mean altar and general coldness of the place are quite unworthy of the sweet Irish anchorite after whom it is called. The alms-house for men in Magdalen Street is served from this church. This is an interesting and puzzling founda-tion. In default of evidence, guessing seems the fashion, and without shame may be resorted to. St. Mary Magdalen's Chapel, on Beckary (afterwards

rededicated to St. Bridget, say in the Norman period),
gives its name to this road. St. Margaret, as patroness,
leads us to expect a hospital for women. It is St.
Margaret, Joan's St. Margaret who is depicted in the bell
cot. In view of the fact that Nicholas Frome arranged
for the charges of the Infirmarius and the Chapel, it may
suggest his date—the middle of the XV Century.
It seems likely that he arranged a hospital here for the
sick women, whether these were dependents on the Abbey
or townsfolk. This has been turned into almshouses
for poor men, ten originally, but now eleven. The
domestic architecture smacks of the Regency. Henry
VIII and Edward VI devoured 110 of these ancient
hospitals, but the two crumbs of the Glastonbury alms-

houses were spared. They
were supported by a reserve
on rents, called the King's
Audit.

With regard to the abbey
hospitality, " Most of what
they did bestow was on the
rich." " It came into a
common proverb to call him
an abbey lubber, that was

Doorway and Holy Water
Stoup in St. Patrick's Chapel

idle, well fed, a long, lewd,
lither, loiterer, that might

work, and would not," says Bishop Pilkington ; but he
adds savagely, " But whether the new monks " (the
landlords), " with their short coats, and almost without
all religion, keeping a shepherd and a dog, where all
good cheer was afore, be worse than the monkish

idolatrous popish creatures, which devised a religion of their own, showing their holiness in their long coats, I leave it to the disputation of the learned." The disputations of the old inmates upon this subject would be more profitable than those of the learned.

These old people in the almshouses receive quarterly 12s. 6d., as subtitutionary grant from the Crown. This is now a ridiculously inadequate sum for them, and if

Piscina and Aumbry in St. Margaret's Almshouse Chapel.

their case were brought before one of the kindliest of monarchs there is no doubt that their plea, which could so reasonably be urged, would awake an immediate response. Wheat varied in the XV and XVI Centuries much more than it does at present: but the sum now allowed to these old people would, in Henry VIII's reign, purchase from four to nine times the amount of wheat they can now buy, so greatly has the purchasing power of money altered. Bishop Latimer, in dismay at the rising dearness of provisions after the Reformation, feared the day might come when a pig would cost a pound. It has come. The pig which fed Latimer and his friends in prison cost only tenpence; but the almshouse people must now save up for their pork, if they ever have any, at the rate of Latimer's fears, *i.e.*, 24 times the price he actually paid. The old pensioners should plead their case. Fifty shillings per annum then, should not be less than a pound a month now, and would not be less, if they appealed rightly.[1]

THE MARKET CROSS

THE lean skimped cross in Confectioner's Gothic, was erected, as is obvious, in 1845. It took the place of a generous old cross, which was pulled down in 1808, to enlarge the street. As the latter survives in prints and postcards, it is worth recording that the Little Monument makes it to have been built long after the dissolution, out of abbey stones. This is hard to believe altogether. It looks, in the prints, like a XV Century cross, but canopied over in Elizabeth's times, and afterwards, but the prints are curiously inaccurate very often. The grotesque figure of a now horseless cavalier, traditionally called Jack Stag, used to crown this compound edifice, and he presided over the Wednesday markets.

The fairs were four in number; they then sunk to none, and have now risen again to two : (1) St. Dunstan's Fair, on May 19th, was in memory of the greatest

[1] Professor Ashley, on the abstract problem, is kind enough to furnish a note agreeing with this estimate of comparisons, viz., that a labourer's subsistence is worth at least four or five times in money what it was at the Dissolution.

of abbots ; (2) Holy Cross Fair was held on Sept. 14th, for there were seven fragments of the true Cross among the relics ; (3) St. Michael's Fair, granted in 1127, by Henry I to the Monastery on the Tor ; (4) A Fair of Our Lady, on her birthday, September 8th. None of these were given in the new description of England in 1701 ; but Holy Cross and St. Michael's Fairs have been revived since, and a stout steed or a fatted calf may still be purchased at these seasons ; besides there are ginger breads and large bull's-eyes for innocents.

ST. JOHN THE BAPTIST'S CHURCH

THIS noble perpendicular church took the place of an earlier Norman one, which was built in cross form, having the tower in the centre. The bases of the old piers still support the later arches to the east. The splendid tower has had its ears cropt, that is, its crocketted pinnacles shortened,[1] but is substantially as it was left in the days of Abbot Selwood. That is to say, it has come down fairly intact from the days of Richard Crookback and Bosworth Fight. It has been fitly compared with St. Cuthbert's Tower at Wells and All Saints' at Wrington. It was being built during the Wars of the Roses, as the tombs of Richard Atwell, and of Joan his wife attest, for the yeoman died just after the Battle of Tewkesbury. Three Atwells, Richard, John and Nicholas, all priests and beneficed in Somerset, were probably the children of this pious pair. The

[1] As may be noticed in the print of the Market Cross.

more interesting tomb of John Camel, the lay chapman,
is earlier.   He is probably related to the John Camel
who was Rector of Ditcheat (1435–58), and he saw the
loss of France, the Rebellion of Cade and the Yorkist
Dominion.   It was probably he who bought the stones
of the great embattled wall to fence the Abbey.

The church has a seal which was in use in the days
of Madcap Hal, and a St. George almsdish, supposed by
some to be acquired from the Walloons, who hated saints.
St. John's once had four side altars, which with their
Lights or Guilds, were swept away in the great pillage.
These were the Lady Altar, St. Katharine's for scholars,
St. George for soldiers, and St. Nicholas for children.
Perhaps these dedications suggest the classes for whom
and by whom the church was built and used.   There
are two mangled mortuary crucifixes outside, which,
being evidence of gross impiety, should be removed
or covered up.   The rood with its Piety, if replaced,
would add much to the appearance of the church.
The communicants are 310.   Concerning the rest of
those who have sepulchral monuments, as concerning
the list of rectors, much search supplies small parcels
of small facts not worth recording in so short a survey.
But the Alleyn altar tomb, in the churchyard, is the
most beautiful monument here.   It is said to be of the
time of Edward IV : but the style, which is transition
from decorated to perpendicular, seems earlier, and the
Alleyns held land in Wayford in the XIV Century, to
which, with a *caveat*, we may assign it.

As this church was in the hands of the Abbey, of
course its endowments were partly plundered with the

main booty, but Edward VI and Bishop Barlow completed the spoliation. The curate of St. John's had three parishes, three churches to serve, and £80 a year, without a house. Fatherly Bishop Ken tried to increase this stipend, but the children of this world were too strong for him. When the Commons Enclosure Act was mooted in 1721, ten acres were set apart for this starveling priest, Master Simon Paget and his successors, who thus got a small share when the common was stolen from the goose ; but the good luck promised by the Flemish almsdish does not extend to the stipend even yet. The clergy also serve St. Patrick's Chapel of the Women's Almshouse, and a mission chapel at Edgarley. The almshouse, with its little chapel, lies within the Abbey, and was founded by the inevitable Beere in 1513. On the entrance are the Tudor arms, the rose with dragon and greyhound supporters. It is the year both of the Expedition to Flanders and of Flodden Field. These arms then show that the young King was a benefactor to this foundation. It seems likelier that the Flemish almsdish came over in this year, appropriated by the English because of St. George.

THE ABBEY GATE

THIS is rather a site than a gate. The original was double bastioned, with an embattled parapet and machicolations, or overhanging top portions, by which hot lead or other dissuasives could be dropped upon the heads of too insistent visitors. The roof was

groined, and a sub-porter lived above the gate, ready
to admit, or repel, as need might be. The crenellated
Stuart window, which the visitor now sees, lit up the
refreshing feasts of the Red Lion Inn, but shed no light
upon the Abbey. The porter's hall, where visitors
waited, was just inside the gate. Above the old battle-
ments poor Whytyng's grey head was displayed in
1539 : but externally little trace remains of the works
which Cade and his company inspired and Nicholas
Frome built. Much of the fabric, and perhaps all of
the foundations, are the same ; but fear and its fortifications, went away at the dissolution along with
wealth. The old ladies of the almshouse are untroubled
by either, and do not miss their first line of defence.

THE GEORGE INN

ABBOT SELWOOD began his long abbacy in the
latter years of Henry VI, and saw the reigns of
Edward IV, Edward V, Richard III, and he died in
1493, the 8th year of Henry VII. He is said to be the
builder of this most interesting Inn. It was not a
place where free feasting was provided to attract worshippers, as some Casino-haunting gentlemen have
imagined. Such incentives to worship were not needed
at the time. On the contrary, it was the Abbot's splendid gift to the Chamberlain, who derived his income
from the hotel bills of the faithful. Had it been a house
of free entertainment, it would not have cured but

Doorway leading to St. Patrick's Chapel.

See page 89.

The George Inn.
See page 90.

completed the "tearful ruin" of this office. The arms
of Edward IV are over the door : to the left being the
arms of St. George of England, and to the right a scraped
shield, which it does not need much audacity to say
must have once held the boar of Richard of Gloucester.
The central coat witnesses to the peace which Selwood
made with the victorious Yorkists ; the erased coat
to the effect of that vaulting ambition. The deep-cut
string courses, the panelled bay, and the octagonal
towers, one hollow for a bell, the bold waywardness
indeed of the whole façade, are most pleasant to the
eye. Inside, plaister and wall paper have done their
worst, and there is nothing archaic to see, until you
reach the vaulted capacious cellars, where you may
learn the usual tales about secret passages, which are
founded upon the fact of secret hiding places being
a necessity of almost all times, but our own : but these
hiding holes were rather that valuables should be passed,
than that men should pass. Still less trustworthy is
the tavern tale that penitents were relegated to the
cellars of Inns, in penance for their youthful follies and
heats of blood. The wine casks and fat butts were never
recommended as fit company for a soul which needed
mortification. Let the dreamers of such ale-washed
theology go to auricular confession themselves, and
declare their own follies and sins to a confessor (who
may have leisure enough to hear them), and they will
soon discover how much more aptly the penance fits
the sin than they had imagined.

The free hospice, where travellers were entertained
humbly, was not the George, but on the site of the White

I

Hart across the way, where " whoso brought the face
of a man brought with him his patent of welcome " :
but if he wished for lordlier cheer, he stopped at the
Georges Yn, and helped to endow the Chamberlain,
who, for some time, was Richard Whytyng, the last of
the Abbots. Similar travellers may still find similar
good cheer, such as they desire ; and the certainty of
a well-aired bed is worth something in the damp air of
this ancient spot. But while they refresh themselves,
let them think kindly of the generations who have come
and gone in this Inn before them—type as it is of man's
guest sojourn in life—and let them remember that there
is no statute of limitations to the IXth Commandment.
It is unfair to bear false witness against men long dead,
but especially against those who struggled pathetically
to do right, even if they only attained to a second best,
and were merely honest Bonifaces, when they should
have been saintly Benedicts.

THE TRIBUNAL

THIS extraordinarily beautiful and simple building
displays the great Abbot Beere's notion of Justice,
being sincere and without flourish. Its plain parapet
and bold cornice give it a severe touch : the bay window
with the six lights (of creation) make it alert, and the
long window of eight lights on the ground floor is to
let the light of blessedness shine upon the unhappy,

for whom human justice was too coarse to do right,
eight being the sign of blessedness. Over the door are
two panels, to give the word of entry in the king's name.
The builder even of King Edgar's Chapel thus proclaims
that the King is the door of civil justice. These panels
are a little puzzling. The one on the right is the
ordinary Tudor twin rose, for the union of the two
houses of York and Lancaster ; but the other panel is
unusual for Henry VII, whose supporters are com-
monly, dexter, a red dragon and sinister, a white greyhound, collared in red. These, however, are a black
bull for Clarence, of the Malmsey butt, whom Henry
claimed to succeed and avenge, and the white lion of
the murdered Earl of March, to whom Richard II had
willed the Crown. This uncertainty of arms points to
an uncertain claim to the throne, so the claim is
strengthened by the Rose of Peace. The place has
served many purposes. It was a seedsman's shop, and
a classical and commercial day-school for young gentlemen. It is now more appropriately a lawyer's office,
where one may hope, some of the original intention is
carried out and justice is aided. The cornice and
windows are like those at Norwood, and in some sort
like the house at Sharpham. In the former the
monogram on the oriel is Selwood's, but the hand of
Beere is visible besides ; but in 1799 Sharpham was
rudely refashioned.

CHALICE WELL

CHILKWELL STREET, formerly Chalkwell Street, is so called from the Chalice well, or Blood Spring, which supplied the town, and possibly the Holy Well at the Old Church. Follow this street, which is at the top of High Street, and you will see the Abbey Barn[1] on your right, and further on a new Roman Catholic Missionary College of the Sacred Heart. This Society took up its abode where the Anchorage Inn had succeeded the Anchorites' huts.[2] Here is the Chalice well, and the green slope behind it is the Chalice Hill, where, in King Peschour's treasury, the Holy Chalice was last seen before it was caught up to the Spiritual City. This is the well which moved even the XVIII Century to faith-healing ; until the faith which cured was derided by the science which could not cure, and the fashion changed. Perhaps these polite missionaries might still turn an honest penny by putting up the water in comely phials, and selling it for healing or baptismal purposes ?

THE TOR

BEHIND Chalice Hill rises the Tor, whose very name is Semitic, and means conspicuous. It is well worth while to climb this old citadel, and to see the rings of old ramparts of the treasure city and the

[1] Page 46.

[2] 1886. They prepare missionaries for hungry places in the North Pacific, etc.

The Tor.

See page 94.

The Spine from the Saviour's Crown of Thorns, now at Stanbrook, near Worcester, one of the Relics of Glastonbury.

(Reproduced by kind permission of the Lady Abbess.)　　　*See page* 102.

wonderful view on all sides. Here they watched for
the Phœnician liners—the men of Dido's race—until
146 B.C. Carthage fell, and the great ships of Tarshish
sailed no more up the Bristol Channel. This is the
hill which Joseph of Arimathæa likened to Tabor, the
Mount of Transfiguration : and here, still, the soul of
man can talk with old law and old prophecy.[1] Here,
in the Second Century, Phaganus and Diruvianus, by
the Lord's revelation, built an oratory in honour of St.
Michael the Archangel of the Church. Here St. Patrick
came with Arnulph and Ogmar, and found the place
tangled with briars. Here they hewed a path through
the brambles and thorns, and rebuilt the Chapel. Here
was still a church and monastery in Henry I time, for
he gave it a fair. But an earthquake overset all the
edifices in 1275, and John de Taunton set to work to
rebuild the church. The shell of his tower still stands :
but its carved statues are gone. St. Michael is seen
weighing a soul against what is " noted in Thy book "
in its favour, and Satan, as usual, trying to cheat. The
woman milking a cow represents the careless worldly
soul getting what it can out of life. The butchery of
Abbot Whytyng, and his two monks, took place here
on Nov. 15th, 1539.

From this hill the eye can notice the limits and
approaches of Avalon. On a clear day the opal and
dove-coloured channel can be seen, and Brent Knoll
rises against the sea-line. This was a British and
Roman camp, and there Ider, one of Arthur's friends,
slew three giants. It guards the estuaries of the rivers,

[1] It is like Mount Tabor too, and very like it.

one can just see. On the right is Edmund's Hill. Turn
south-east and you look to Edgarley, where fiery
little Edgar had a house, and lived with the most
lovely Elsruet or Aelgifu, who murdered young
Edward.[1]

There was St. Dunstan's Chapel, and there Alfred
fought with the Danes. Look to the north and north-
west and see the Mendip, the old home of lead mines
and oppression. There beyond Edgarley is the road
to West Pennard, along which Sir Launcelot followed
dead Guinevere ; and centuries afterwards Edward I
came to do honour to King Arthur. What march and
countermarch has been watched from this spot : approaches of pirates, Welsh tributaries with wolves' heads
for Edgar, Irish devotees, Danes, Lancastrians, rebels,
Roundheads ! The great spire of the Abbey, seen from
this summit, must have risen to the sea-line, and its
music have been faintly and faerily audible here. This
hill shows us " The holyest erth of England," as an old
writer calls it. It is still a land of dreams. The aged
people tell of fairies flitting like bats, and clinging to
the ruins, of moving lights and walking spirits. The
very cattle within sight of the Tor, and it can be seen
from unimaginable distances, try to approach it on
Christmas Eve. " They must be well penned in to
keep them back." It is no common earth here, which
appeals to eye and heart so mysteriously, in this land
of dreams.

But dreams apart, as we look over this old inheritance and see the lands so rich in story, the question

[1] Gaimar's Chronicle.

rises, whether the men of old got more out of life than
we do ? *Plus viæ*, more whisking about, as the Latin
poet says, does not mean the same as *plus vitæ*, more
of life. Take the very land and water before our eyes.
The rivers were full of salmon, with fist-thick tails.
There were bee-farms, yielding quarts of honey and
thousands of wax candles—the paschal candle alone
weighed close on a hundred weight. There were vine-
yards—two at Glastonbury, one at Meare, and another
at Pamborrow. There were water-ways and many
mills, for grinding and fulling. There was much
weaving, spinning, casting, hammer-work, painting,
jewelry, tapestry, music and designing. 2,000 eels came
from the bucks at Sowy. The great lake at Meare was
full of large pike, bream perch and roach. The parks
were full of deer—400 usually at Sharpham, the moors
with wild fowl, and the pools with swans. Pageantry is a
poor substitute for life, no doubt ; but an uncommonly
good sauce. The men whose chimneys one sees from
the Tor have the strenuous labour of their fathers, and,
if they have less of fear, have more of anxiety. Yet
how uncoloured is their existence in comparison, and
how dull their outlook, without this pageantry which
was not shut up in halls, but was public and common !
The very alms of the Abbey, some £30 and more of
our money in the week, were not given so unwisely as
some would make out. If food was given to all strangers
in the name of Christ the Stranger, those who were no
strangers had to account for their presence at the
almonry and their need. In educational matters the
Abbey was a ladder for such as had agility and head

to climb to great offices. In higher matters still, religious education was given in the best and only right way, by interesting the people. It was not imparted to them by coarse and forceful machinery, but joyfully and richly ; not through one over-worked sense, ear-gate, but by that and by every other gate to the soul. Thus the Abbey was also a spiritual ladder from the deeps of man's nature to the heights of God's mercy : and His highest mercy is Himself.

NOTE ON THE RELICS

THE great collectors for the Abbey were Kings Ethelstan, Edmund the Elder, and Edgar ; the Thanes Elnoth, Alfar, Ethelstan, Elwin ; Earl Elstan, Archbishop Poppa of Treves, Bishops Britwold of Wincester, Britwin of Wells, Saifrid of Chichester, Henry de Blois, Abbot Tictan, Eustace the Prior, Aelswita a noble matron, and Adam de Sodbury. The relics being often very small, and contained many in one precious case, often got separated from their labels and confused, particularly if the cases were removed quickly. The chip of stone from Isaiah's tomb, a small bone of Daniel, a fragment of Manna, of Moses' rod and of the three holy children, and six little dice-like gold mosaics from the Temple would go into less space than do the printed words enumerating them. A small reliquary of St. Gregory contained one or two of our Saviour's hairs, crumbs of the barley loaf, threads from the purple robe and from His seamless coat, a fragment of the sponge on the reed, flakes of stone from Golgoth and Calvary, 7 portions of the True Cross. A water pot from Cana was also among the relics. One spine from the Crown of Thorns was another relic much prized, and part of Our Lady's robe, hair, and even milk. All the Apostles were represented. Some hairs of St. Peter's beard and two of his teeth were in crystals. St. Paul, St. Stephen, St. Mary Magdalen's hair, relics of the Holy Innocents, of all the Apostles, and even a fragment of Our Lady's flower, the lily she held at the Annunciation, were shown. The Evangelists all had bones here and St. John Baptist the same. SS. Cyprian, Jerome, Ambrose, Gregory and other Fathers were represented ; Popes Clement, Calixtus and the body of Urban I also. Of St. George there were an arm, two bones, some hair and fragments, of St. Augustine of England, dust. There were nineteen bones of St. Vincent, and some of St. Margaret, with her sandals, King Edmund the Martyr's shirt, very many things of St. Thomas, cowl, linen stained with blood, cloak, hair shirt and so on, St. Christopher's crown, St. Philip's jaw, with teeth in it, St. Peter's staff and a stole, St. Oswald's shoulder and hand ; relics of St. Edmund, St. Osmund of Sarum and St. Alban—these were all in the feretories. Strangely enough the Northern Saints were well represented, contributed by King Ethelstan. Aidan, Bede, Benedict Biscop and Cuthbert were there piece-meal. Hilda and Guthlac, Birinus, Martin, Cosmas and Damian, Petroc and Welsh or Cornish Saints of wonderful names, gave subdivided honours. In fact the very mention is

wearisome of the glorious companies, noble armies, and
goodly fellowships, who helped to make up the dust of
Glastonbury.   Sodbury's present of two bones of St.
Katharine, with oil and other remains, accounts for
and dates her prominent place in the seal.   The " portion of St. Paulinus' finger " may be that now in the
Museum.   St. Helena's arm, with flesh still on it, was
treasured here, and, " although loss of record has made
many names unknown to us, the relics are stored up
in our keeping.   Although our knowledge of them
comes short, they are enjoying at large the knowledge
and sight of God," says John of Glaston, with pious
simplicity.   That, perhaps, is the key of what is a little
puzzling to modern people in this sincere enthusiasm
for relics, which have no message for most of us.   " Our
one aim and desire," he would tell us, " is to behold
God, to see the King in His beauty.   Here are those
who actually do this great thing.   Give us anything
that will join us to them, and number us with these
saints in this glory everlasting."   Surely a reasonable
habit of mind would make us reply, that we cannot
grudge to others what we are too self-sufficient to need
in our own lives ?   The cruel brutality of the Commissioners, who burnt the bones of the masters of the
holy life, cannot be excused on any pleas of mere
unbelief.

Of the kings who are buried here, Hoel, grandfather
of Constantine, Arthur, Kentwin the two Edmunds,
Ethelstan, Edgar, and an older British king, Aberdare,
make up eight.   Twenty-nine bishops and abbots, with
Thanes and Earls, and lesser Barons innumerable, swell

the list, before we even reach God's common people. These folk were not (save St. Edgar) worshipped. They had incited no one to ask for their prayers ; yet their tombs were destroyed, and their dust defiled. Poor Guinevere's golden hair was as little respected as the lock from Her head, whom all generations call blessed. St. Joseph of Arimathæa is happy at least in this, that his resting-place has escaped both the honours and the dishonours of more than fifty generations. The hand that touched the feet of God is still safe from the shrine, the bonfire, or—worse still—the Museum.

THE SEAL

THIS seal, of the time of Abbot John Chinnock, is introduced to show the Abbey Spire. There are several other points of interest about it. The original silver seal is lost, melted, no doubt, in some thieves' pot. It had two sides to it. On the one, three masculine saints, Patrick, Dunstan and Benignus, with the legend, *Confirmant has res + scripti pontifices tres*—the holy bishops three, assurance give to thee. The other has three women saints, St. Katharine with her wheel, Our Lady with the Word of God and a vase of roses in the centre, and St. Margaret with her Dragon. The jingle on this is *Testis adest isti, scripto pia genetrix Xti—Glastonie*—God's gentle Mother dear, as witness too is here, Glastonbury. Relics of St. Katharine were brought by Adam de Sodbury both to the Abbey and St. John's. St. Margaret's sandals and a bone of her, were treasured in St. Mary's. The architecture on the seal is XV Century, and gives, perhaps, some notions of the Chapter-house, which this Abbot finished.

The seal is taken from the submission of Abbot Whytyng, and all the Convent to the Oath of Supremacy.

THE RELIC OF THE HOLY THORN

BY the courtesy of the Lady Abbess of Stanbrook, near Worcester, a Benedictine House, the reader can see a picture of what claims to be one of Glastonbury's most interesting relics, a thorn from the Redeemer's Crown. This is now at Stanbrook.

The relic and reliquary were separately presented to the Altar of Our Lady of Power in the Chapel of the Holy Rosary in London in the XVII Century. The former was the gift of Peter Warnford, a secular priest, who brought it to the Community when he became a Benedictine. He died in 1657. The latter was the gift of " Mr. Augustine Stocker to the Ladye of Power." At the time of Oates' plot, the registers of this Sodality were, unfortunately, destroyed and the story of how the relic was saved in 1539, and how it passed into Warnford's hands, is not known. The Warnford, or Warnesford, family was well known in Somerset, John being Sub-dean of Wells at the end of the XV Century. Edmund and Edward (*milites*) held lands in the XVII Century in the Archdeaconry of Wells. The Stockers held land at Chilcompton, after Philip and Mary, and one of these, a Sir John, was patron of the ex-abbey living of Lympsham. A further account of the relic

Statue of Abbot William Vigor, in the
Abbot's Kitchen.

See page 103.

The Holy Thorn.
See page 105.

may be seen in M. Fleury's Relics of the Passion, and
Fr. Morris' Article in the *Month* for August, 1882. The
wonder is not that one or two out of the long list of
relics were preserved by reverent hands, but that so few
are now to be found with any claim to examine. This
one has the seal of the late Bishop Ullathorne. In com-
paring the lists of relics, this sacred thorn does not
seem to have been at Glastonbury before the XIV
Century. It is first mentioned by John of Glastonbury.

ABBOT WILLIAM VIGOR

THE figure placed in the Abbot's kitchen in A.D.
1780 is remarkably well preserved. The mitre,
unjewelled, makes it obviously later than the year 1190,
when the mitre was given to the Abbots of Glastonbury. The beard gives the date as early XIII Century.
The only possible Abbot would be William Vigor for
this figure, for Savaric was buried at Bath, Jocelin at
Wells, Pike at Rome, and the first mitred Abbot, Henry
de Soliaco, at Worcester. William Vigor was, it almost
goes without saying, a gentleman of the county, from
the Hemington de Vigors, or de Victors. His name
comes in the submission to Savaric, who had reduced
the rebel monks with fasting and flagellation. William
was chosen at the *renovatio* in 1219, when the Abbey
escaped from the See, and had its privileges confirmed
by Pope Honorius III, of crusading memory. The first
act of Abbot William (St. Francis is still alive) was to
pour out his treasures into the hands of the poor. Next
he strengthened the Convent ale, re-tithed the corn for

the brethren, enriched the Prior's office and that of
hosteller, farmerer, gardener and butler, for devout
celebration of his own anniversary. He gave the offer-
ings on the Assumption and Our Lady's Birthday to the
Sacristy of the Lady Chapel, and was mindful of the
sick. He died on Sept. 18th, 1223, and was buried in the
Chapter House, in the south part. Thus he lived to
the reign of Pandulf, and attended the Council of Oxford,
where a deacon, who out of love of a Jewess had
renounced Christ, was degraded, and afterwards burnt ;
also a man and woman who claimed to be Our Lord and
the Blessed Virgin, were " closed up betweene two walles
of stone, where they ended their liues in misery." Four
days before William died, there was a great thunder-
storm, with great floods and winds, which perhaps
hastened his end. *Requiescat !*

ABBOT WHYTYNG'S CHASUBLE[1]

THIS exquisitely worked vestment, which is now
in St. John's Church, was actually cut, pieced and
used as a carpet in St. John's Church. Considering
the general shape, as evidenced by the cuts and

[1] Since 1912 this *Vestment* (?) has been much restored, and is
now preserved in a glass case fixed to the wall of the north aisle
of St. John's Church. Further investigation appears to prove
it to have been a Pall. It is officially described as " *A Pall made
from a Cope formerly in use in this church Ca.* 1500." In any
case it is a remarkable survival. In 1909 it was in the Museum !
This *Pall* measures 10 ft. × 5 ft. The material is brown velvet,
with a full length blue velvet cross ; richly embroidered, in the
centre is a figure of Our Lady, crowned, and surrounded by
angels and rays of glory.

joining, it becomes fairly certain that it was a Gothic chasuble, such as would fit a tall man, rather than a cope, as it is often described, or a dalmatic, as we should expect. It is pathetically interesting both as the sole surviving relic of that rich vestry, the robe of the unhappiest of the abbots and as the evidence of gross barbarity, which could trample on such flowers of art.

THE HOLY THORN

THE story of the holy thorn, St. Joseph's staff, rests frankly upon botany and tradition alone. It is not mentioned in mediæval writers.

In the XVII Century, Bishop Godfrey Goodman thought the tree to be aged, " much about the time of the dissolution of the Abbey." It must be confessed that Abbey authors neither mention this thorn nor the walnut which opened on St. John's day. But the Commissioners at the dissolution sent specimens of the thorn to King Henry VIII, and the Prior of Maiden Bradley assured them that it was actually found to flower at Christmas. The present holy thorn, not now on Wirriall but inside the northern gate of the Abbey, cannot be much more than a century and a half old, but older specimens are found about Somerset. Gerarde discreetly withdrew from the controversies which raged about this thorn in Elizabeth's time ; and Fuller weakly suggested that the sly monks made it to flower by warm waterings. Its habits have " disproved " Protestantism, Socinianism and Deism in turn, and the indignant Sectaries cut it down, in hope that its vexatious arguments would thus cease, which they did not. It is certainly a Mediterranean thorn, and comes, in its inception, quite possibly from the Holy Land. It has an immense inherent vitality about it. Some sprays of blossom put in a church at Christmas retained their sweetness till Candlemas, and seemingly dead twigs have often burgeoned vigorously. Thus there is nothing improbable in the story that St. Joseph had a staff of this tree, that he left it in the ground, and that it grew and blossomed always at Christmas.

PRINTED IN GREAT BRITAIN AT THE PITMAN PRESS, BATH
(8183w)